A voyage through
BRITTANY

Text:

SERGE DUIGOU

English translator:

JEAN-PAUL TRUDE

jos,
GROUPE ★ EDITOR

Although départements have existed for over two hundred years, in Brittany they will never be the most pertinent geographical entity. First and foremost the Breton sees himself as coming from a particular pays, each having its own particular cultural and historical identity.

During the Ancient Regime bishoprics were the first main reference for the population. In the dioceses of Lower-Brittany, one was Cornouaillais (Quimper), Léonard (Saint-Pol-de-Léon), Vannetais (Vannes), Trégorois (Tréguier), and each spoke their own local variant of the Breton language.

But what differences could exist in each bishopric ! By crossing some insignificant stream and arriving at the first farm, one would have the surprise of finding that the costume and headdress had changed. One had crossed from one *pays* to another. Around the *pays* Glazik of the capital itself (Quimper), the Cornouaille region has its *pays* Porzay, the Crozon Peninsula, the *pays* Bigouden, the *pays* Fouesnantais, and others less well-known - like the *pays* Mélénik -, or those of a single parish (Plougastel-Daoulas).

A *pays* is generally the region of economic and cultural influence around an important market town. The population from local parishes would meet on regular market and fair days and realized in time that they shared a common destiny. This led to common dress, language (Breton or Gallo dialects), culinary, musical (instruments, song and dance) traditions, as well as a local style of building and furniture. In time, this became a local mentality, a psychology, a way of life, a deep down "local conscientiousness". A source of competition and often outright rivalry between neighbouring pays, these differences have led to a typology recognized by everybody. The Léon, austere "land of priests", is so different from its neighbouring Trégor, more loving of the things of life, and from the *pays* Bigouden, land of the caracoling "cheval d'orgueil".

The *pays* is destined to become an economically important entity and in the long term even assume a real administrative identity. The inhabitants of Finistère will not complain, for they have always considered themselves as Léonards in the north and Cornouaillais in the south. Likewise for the inhabitants of the *pays* of Redon, straddling three départements and two administrative regions!

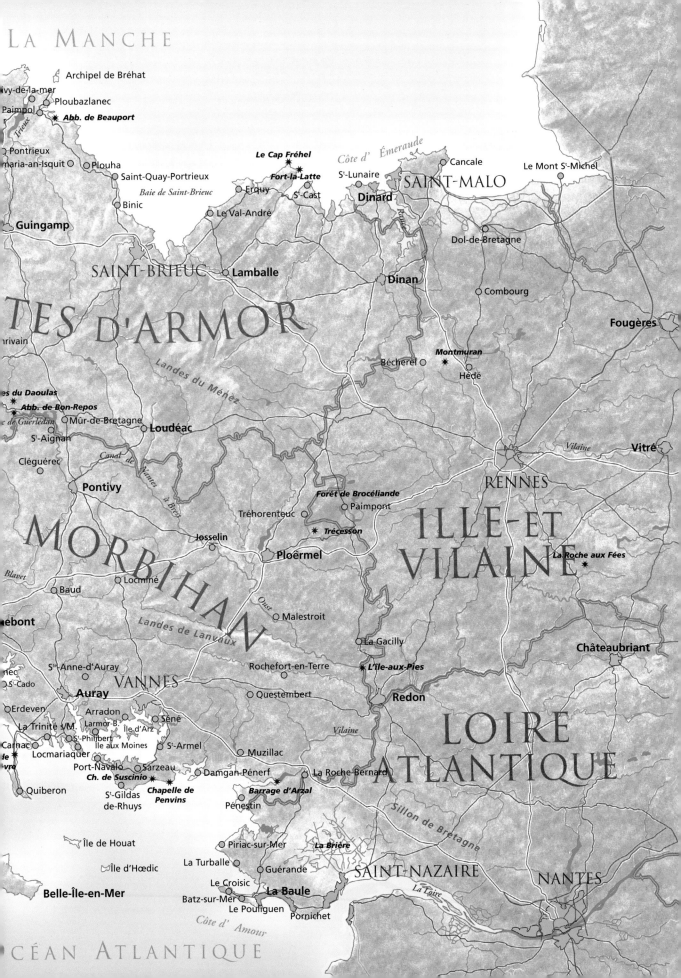

L'ARGOAT *

It would be an injustice to think of Brittany as only a indented coast with its estuaries and islands, for it is difficult to remain insensitive to the poetic charm of the inland parts of the peninsula.

Do not be misled by the word "argoat": the land of woods. This was true in the Middle Ages. Since then, monasteries, the local parishes and the French Navy have been responsible for the forest's decline, although it has not completely disappeared.

The clearings and thickets of Brittany most famous forest, Brocéliande (commonly called Paimpont), still echo with the adventures of Merlin and the fairy Viviane.

The attraction of the Argoat is in its diversity of landscapes, rocks and buildings. Although the highest point of the Monts d'Arrée (Arrée Mountains) and the Montagnes Noires (Black Mountains) is only 384 m, modesty and monotony are not synonymous. In the heart of the peninsula, the Nantes to Brest canal weaves its quiet way through a variety of landscapes, alternating between farmland, sometimes victim of excessive regrouping, and vast areas of wild moorland and peat-bogs.

In this heartland are set the fundamental milestones of Breton history, incarnated, for example, by the impressive castles of the Rohan family in Josselin and Pontivy. Here also are the jewels in the Breton crown, the chapels of Saint Fiacre and Sainte Barbe in Faouët, the churches of Kernascléden and Queven, the parish closes of Sizun and Commana, a hundred other sanctuaries, even more manor houses, and how many fountains and megalithic standing stones and monuments? Also villages, Moncontour, Rochefort-en-Terre, Lizio, with their somewhat old-fashion charm, their provincial restful calm, far from the feverish coast.

A land of contrasts: Loudéac is at the forefront in agriculture and food products, Bécherel has created itself an image as the town of books. The nuclear power station of Brennilis - in the process of being dismantled - built its concrete towers on the edges of Yeun Elez, the marsh that hides one of the gateways to Hell!

A land of roots and the myths of Brittany's past. Brocéliande and the Arthurian legends, Carhaix and the Gallo-Roman past of Armorica, and everywhere, the founder saints, unknown in Rome, who crossed from mainland Britain to christianize the region during the late Middle Ages.

In the town of Spezet, one can tell from the shop signs that they speak Breton. All over the "Mountain", the area around Carhaix, they dance the gavotte in the most authentic "fest-noz" (night festivals) of the entire peninsula. Despite, or perhaps because of its economic and demographic problems (some areas are being deserted by the population), the Argoat is the Breton heart of modern Brittany.

* The land of woods.

L'ARMOR *

*The land of the sea. Stormy or calm; a sea of rocky coasts and sheltered beaches;
a sea that carves estuaries, also called rias or abers, where the bracing sea air
and the mildness of the fields meet and blend in a subtle and ever-changing mix.*

A sea falsely tamed in the Morbihan Gulf, the gem of the southern coast. A sea of cliffs and coastal marshes, with ledges, crevices and coastal marshland offering refuge for nesting birds.

And beyond, the islands. Ushant the wild, Sein the solitary, Bréhat the luxuriant, the Glénan archipelago with its emerald lagoon. And those proud guardians, the off-shore lighthouses, Ar Men, Kereon, La Vieille, who have written some of the glorious and tragic pages of maritime history.

A provider sea, the work place for thousands of fishermen, oyster farmers, seaweed gatherers, constantly struggling for survival against competition, European rules and regulations, the scarcity of resources. Lorient and Concarneau, the Bigouden ports, do more than resist in a context full of incertitude. Fishing boats returning to port in the late afternoon and the fish and crustaceans sold by auction in the fish market, teaches one more about the Bretons than all the books in the world.

A cruel sea, of shipwrecks, of wreck-robbers of the past, and at the same time, a sea of daily heroism, of rescue services on constant alert. A sea for solitary sailors, their eyes filled with dreams. Isn't that so Eric Tabarly ?

L'Armor is not limited to the coastal fringe, but includes areas that are more or less influenced by the sea. Like Quimper on the River Odet, Landerneau on the Elorn, Lannion on the Léguer, many Breton towns were established at the end of an estuary, where the limit of the tide allowed a ford or a bridge to be built and a commercial harbour to develop.

Brittany would not be Brittany without the ocean that carves it, whips it, feeds it. Channel to the north, Iroise to the west and Atlantic to the south, each maritime facade has its own identity, its own "climate". Since time began, be it history, or the legends of the town of Ys and Tristan and Iseut, the peninsula has been intimately entwined by the liquid element of the sea.

Two large ports developed during the reign of Louis XIV, le Ponant at Brest and the India Company at Lorient. The sea and its numerous associated activities brought fame and fortune to Saint-Malo, town of privateers, and also to Nantes, retrospective champion of the somewhat shameful business of slave trading.

The sea has forged and will continue to forge the personality of Brittany… and the Bretons.

* The land of the sea.

Finistère

A VOYAGE THROUGH BRITTANY

The Finistère is a land of paradoxes. Hemmed in by the sea on three sides, it is the France's most agricultural département. Legends of the town of Ys and the Ile Longue nuclear submarine base coexist. The Finistèriens are solidly anchored to their identity, to such a degree that the surviving traditional Bigouden headdresses have now become a symbol for the whole of Brittany. But what diversity! Between the rigorous Léonard and the more carefree Cornouaillais, between the inhabitants of Brest, the new, the French, and Quimper, the historical, the Breton. They all agree though, that they live in a region that is unequaled anywhere.

LE CONQUET

In the 16th century Le Conquet was a Breton port of European importance. Not only was it a port of call for the numerous ships rounding the Brittany headland, it was the home port of an impressive fleet of merchant vessels. Merchant captains traded along the Atlantic coast in a varied freight of wine, cereals, salt, dried fish, canvas. Moreover, a local cartographic workshop made the name of Le Conquet known throughout the maritime and scientific world.

With its fine corbelled tower overlooking the estuary, the 16th century maison des Seigneurs is a reminder of this rich past.

The port's present-day fleet of fishing boats catch mainly devilfish, turbot, conger eels, crayfish, edible crab and spider crabs. Opposite the harbour is the Kermorvan headland, with its 1849 lighthouse. To the south, this small peninsula shelters the popular Blancs Sablons (white sands) beach.

The Kermorvan headland and its lighthouse.

Blancs Sablons beach.

SAINT-MATHIEU POINT

The view alone from the prow of Saint-Mathieu Point, is reason enough to linger here. Since the 15th century monks have worked and prayed here. There are impressive remains of the Benedictine abbey, which according to tradition, was set up by Saint Tanguy, despite him being responsible for the murder of his own sister, Sainte Haude. The early Gothic style columns and arches make rather curious neighbours for the 54 metre-high lighthouse, built in 1835.

Bertheaume Fort

This setting, an island at the entrance to the Brest Roadstead, destined it to fortified military use. It has been fortified since the Middle Ages, but the present fort was built by Vauban during the reign of Louis XIV, when artillery was installed. From 1870 onwards it was dismantled, but was used by the Germans during the Second World War for gun emplacements. The rock protects the popular beaches of Trégana and Trez-Hir from the northeasterly winds.

*The wild splendour of Penn Point
on the island of Ushant.*

ISLAND OF USHANT

A little over a thousand inhabitants share the one thousand five hundred and sixty hectares of the island of Ushant, an advanced sentry post of the French coasts between the Channel and the Atlantic Ocean.

A kingdom of storms, jagged rocks and impressive cliffs, the island's beauty is breath-taking. The north coast in particular, from Pern Point to Cadoran Point, is constantly pounded by a never resting sea.

The Stiff (one of the oldest in France) and Creac'h lighthouses on the island, and Nividic, Kéréon and Jument lighthouses at sea are never to many to guide shipping around some of the world's most dangerous waters.

Whilst the Ushant women farmed the land and kept the sheep, the men went to sea and were often absent for long periods. As with many island societies, it is an island of women. An island where bereavement was so frequent that the tradition black headdress imposed itself over the one worn in happier times. As is often the case for those who lost their lives at sea, there was no body at the funeral. It was replaced by a symbolic wax cross. This ceremony and its cross (ceased since 1962) was called *proella* ("the homecoming of souls" - translator's note).

Since 1968 Ushant is part of the Armorique Regional Nature Park. In order to try and insure its economic survival and protect its natural resources and scenery, Unesco has classed the island as a World Biosphere Reserve. Ushant's wild and harsh authenticity leaves no one indifferent.

ISLAND OF MOLÈNE

In the heart of its archipelago, made up of several islands devoted to nature conservation, Molène's ninety hectares has about two hundred and fifty inhabitants. The origin of its name - Moal Enez in Breton means the "bald island" - needs no comment. Its small fleet of boats fish for crustaceans, lobster and crayfish. Tourism is an important extra activity for its courageous population who have remained faithful to solar time and continue to live on an island which has been inhabited since prehistoric times. Seaweed gatherers from the Léonard coast still come here to harvest laminar seaweeds.

The shipwrecked

The 16th of June 1896 was a tragic date. That night, in thick fog, the British liner "Drummond Castle", returning from a cruise to the Cape, ran aground on rocks to the west of Molène and sank in four minutes. There were only three survivors ; two hundred and forty three people lost their lives. The inhabitants of Ushant and Molène watched over the bodies before burying them. As a sign of gratitude, the English financed the building of Ushant's church belfry.

BREST

Tonnerre de Brest

The "Tonnerre de Brest" was a canon shot informing the Brestois that someone had escaped from the prison. An important reward was offered for his capture. The Brest prison, housed in a building of the naval dockyards, was renowned for its severity.

Brest suffered much destruction during the last war but with determination and courage has reestablished its civil and military importance. It is Finistère's largest town (160,000 inhabitants). It is the home of the Préfecture maritime and l'Université de Bretagne Occidentale (West Brittany University) created in 1960. It is one of western France's most dynamic towns.

The great drawbridge, the Tanguy tower and the Naval Dockyard.

The position of the small town on the inner deep water roadstead watching over the Atlantic Ocean, persuaded Richelieu and later Colbert to establish an important naval dockyard on the banks of the Penfeld River.

During the 18th century naval vessels set out from here to almost every destination in the world. The navy and its officers were the town's blazing glory. The town was at its apogee.

The rue de Siam and Marta Pan's sculpture-fountains.

The future of Brest lays in the outer port on the roadstead, where the "Charles de Gaulle", France's first nuclear powered aircraft carrier, was launched. It has become a symbol of high technology for a town turned more and more towards the future.

The Place de la Liberté, the War Memorial (1958) and the rue de Siam. On the right, Saint-Louis church (1957).

In the 12th century a fort already existed, built on a rocky promontory at the mouth of the Penfeld River. Over time, as a keep and curtain walls were added, the castle was extended, modernized and made more and more impregnable. In the 15th century, two impressive towers were added, flanking the main entrance gate and the drawbridge.

The Tanguy tower, built in the 14th century on the bank opposite the castle, was for some time the seat of the then local justice authorities. Since 1964 it houses an historical museum.

Following the massive destruction during the period 1940-1944, the charm of former streets and squares - Ah! the left bank of the Penfeld, Recouvrance de Mac Orlan and its sailors out on the town - was lost. Having decided to rebuild the town in a rational way, albeit sometimes with a certain lack of imagination concerning housing, Brest has never the less many fine examples of modern urban development.

Some examples are: the reinforced steel and concrete drawbridge, inaugurated in 1954; the severe modern beauty of the Saint-Louis church, with its ochre coloured Lagonna stone married with concrete; the rue de Siam and its futuristic fountains; the Place de la Liberté, overlooked by the 1961 modern town hall.

The tramway, with its lime green livery and its streamlined elegance has become very popular with the Brestois. The new 14.3 km-long tramway, with its 27 stations, crosses the town from east to west from Plouzané to Gouesnou and Guipavas in 38 minutes.

Océanopolis

With its modern architectural design in the form of a crab, Océanopolis is a landmark next to the Moulin Blanc marina. Its aquariums, public exhibitions, tanks, media centre and research laboratories are all dedicated to the discovery of the fascinating mysteries of the sea, this "world of silence".

THE BREST ROADSTEAD

The Brest roadstead is a magnificent protected stretch of water which opens out to sea through a narrow channel (Le Goulet), which is peppered with wrecks of all ages. It is the regular setting for magnificent marine heritage and tall ships festivals.

Passing Petit Minou Point lighthouse, a three-master in full sail.

"La Recouvrance". The construction of this schooner began in 1961 in the Guip dockyard. It was launched in 1992 during the "Brest 92" marine heritage festival.

During these festivals, all kinds of traditional sailing boats, schooners, three-masters, both merchant and military, parade in full sail, a colourful and nostalgic reminder of our marine heritage.

But the roadstead is also the setting for many divers sea-related activities which include oyster and fish farming and scallop shell harvesting. There is also the Ile Longue, now joined to the mainland, whose imposing military installations are the base of the French Navy's nuclear submarine force.

Between Plougastel-Daoulas and Relecq-Kerhuon, the Iroise Bridge, inaugurated on the 12 July 1994.

Scallop fishing (coquille St-Jacques)

Fished on the sand banks of the Saint-Brieuc Bay and the Brest roadstead, this variety of scallop differs from others by its size (minimum 102 mm). It can be eaten fried in butter or "flambée".

The Plougastel-Daoulas calvary and its hieratic figures.

PLOUGASTEL-DAOULAS

Famous for its strawberry and tomato growing, the Plougastel-Daoulas peninsula is also the setting for many charming little chapels hidden in its wooded landscape. But it is especially renown for its monumental calvary, built after the Plague epidemic of 1598. Its 180 figures of Kersanton granite were carefully restored following damage during the last war.

Plougastel strawberries

The little red fruit, imported from South America in the second half of the 17th century by the botanist Frézier, was to make the area famous. Exported to Great Britain from the middle of the 19th century onwards, the strawberry brought wealth to the peninsula, as does the growing of tomatoes and flowers, which began later.

LANDERNEAU

At the junction between the Cornouaille and Léon regions, Landerneau has one of Europe's rare inhabited bridges, the Rohan Bridge, named after the former local lords. Amongst some of the town's other charms are the churches of Saint-Houardon and Saint-Thomas and the fine Logonna stone-built town houses.

The Legend of the Landerneau moon

Bored with the splendors of the Sun King's court, a Breton gentleman exclaimed: "The Landerneau moon is bigger than the one at Versailles". He meant by that the copper moon-shaped weathercock on the Saint-Houardon church spire. Thus the Landerneau moon became a legend.

THE ABERS

From the Aber Wrac'h, in the north, to the Aber Ildut in the south, not forgetting the Aber Benoît, the Abers *pays* is a geographical region modeled by wide estuaries and short rivers. Formerly an important centre of coastal trading, it is now the Breton capital of seaweed gathering activities.

The beach on the estuary of the Aber-Benoit.

The seaweed gatherer's "Scoubidou"

The "scoubidou" is a big corkscrew-like hook attached to a crane which can rip up seaweed in up to 5 metres of water. Once the hook hoisted, a single sailor on board just rotates the contraption in the opposite direction to free the long laminar (Laminaria digitata) seaweed and heaps them up on the boat's deck. This seaweed, once ashore and dried, is sent to factories where alginates are extracted for use in the food and pharmaceutical industries.

Aber-Wrac'h harbour.

Three kilometres out to sea stands the Four lighthouse (built on a rock in 1873) marking the separation between the Channel and the Atlantic Ocean.

The Amoco Cadiz

On the 20th of March 1978, the giant petrol tanker, the Amoco Cadiz, in difficulty, dropped its anchor as a last resort, dragged its 20.5 ton anchor in the strong winds and currents (breaking the anchor's points), ran aground near the Men Goulven rocks, 1.100 metres east-north-east of the Corn Carhai lighthouse, causing one of the century's most important oil spills.

Pontusval Point lighthouse in the setting sun.

On the Ile Vierge, on the coast near Plouguerneau, stand two lighthouses: the older one (and the smallest) built in 1845, and the more recent built in 1897.

The latter, 82.5 metres high, is Europe's tallest lighthouse, and world's tallest stone-built one. 325 steps lead up to the lantern.

According to tradition, it used to be considered unwise for a sailor to be shipwrecked on the coast between Plouguerneau and Plounénour-Trez, on this coast of "pagans", whose reputation was so bad. The inhabitants of the region had the reputation for being wreck-robbers, or even shipwreckers. Going "to the wreck" was their favorite pastime. The numerous lighthouses and buoys that now punctuate this dangerous coast are proof that such times have long since disappeared. At the foot of a mass of rocks, the picturesque village of Menez Ham near Kerlouan is more a reminder of the times of the farmer-seaweed gatherer.

Notre-Dame du Folgoët

The basilica of Folgoët owes it existence to a very charming story: in the middle of the 14th century a poor simpleton called Salaün lived there. The only thing he could say was "Ave Maria", two words he repeated all day long whilst begging or swinging from branch to branch in the trees. When he died he was buried in his wood. Some time afterwards astonishing news spread through the whole region: a lis had miraculously grown on the abandoned tomb and the words AVE MARIA were carved in letters of gold. Crowds came to see the miracles, and thus began the traditional pilgrimage, still carried on to this day.

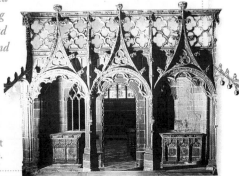

15th century rood-loft in fine pierced Kersanton stone.

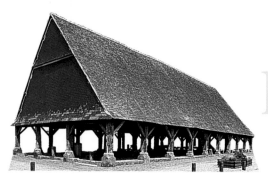

PLOUESCAT

Built by a Baron of Kerouzéré in the 15th century, the Plouescat covered market still has its magnificent oak structure. The local baron received taxes on the goods and animals sold at the market. The indented coast, marked by rocks and reefs, has a surprise in stall for the visitor. In Kernic Bay, a passage grave, originally built in a field, is now on the beach, a witness to the rise in sea level since Neolithic times.

CLÉDER

On the Cléder coast, at Amiets and near Kerfissien, two watch posts still remain. In order to keep watch and defend the coast against the English menace, Louis XIV and his naval engineer Vauban, decided to build these installations, recognizable by their stone roofs. They housed either signal masts or gun batteries. They were later used by the customs, hence the name they are given today "customs house".

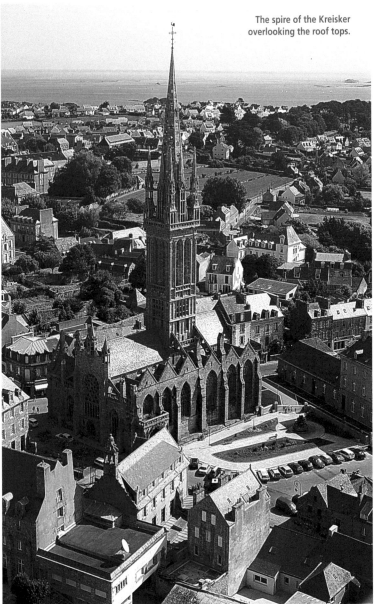

The spire of the Kreisker overlooking the roof tops.

The remarkable edifice of the cathedral, dedicated to Pol Aurélien.

This 6th century bronze bell is said to have been offered to Saint Paul by Count Withur.

SAINT-POL-DE-LÉON

Saint-Pol-de-Léon, the centre of the so called "golden belt", was, until the Revolution, the seat of the bishopric of Saint Paul Aurélien. The town still has some of its bygone charm and an elegant Gothic cathedral. Inside the cathedral one immediately notices the harmony of the late 15th century transept rose-window and the macabre tradition of skull boxes bearing the deceased's name.

The town boasts an equally impressive second church, the Notre-Dame du Kreisker chapel, used for the town's assembly before the Revolution. The fine and exceptional 79 metre-high spire is a esthetic and technical masterpiece of Gothic architecture.

Artichokes

Because of its mild climate and rich soil the coastal region around Saint-Pol-de-Léon was known as the "golden belt". The artichokes, cauliflowers and shallots grown here represent three quarters of France's production. In order to improve the sales and distribution of their produce, local farmers created an auction market in Saint-Pol-de-Léon and a deep water port in Roscoff.

Sainte Apolline

Apolline was martyred at Alexandria in 249. According to legend, having refused to worship idols, her teeth were pulled out with pliers, and seeing the stake that awaited her, she threw herself into the flames. She became the patron saint of "tooth pullers".

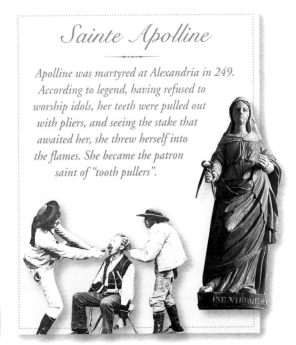

ROSCOFF

What a turbulent past Roscoff has! This "old haunt of pirates and privateers" spent its time either fighting the English or trading along the Atlantic coast, before becoming a base for smuggling wine, spirits and tea to England. Local merchants became rich and demonstrated their wealth by financing the building of the Notre-Dame-de-Croaz-Batz church in 1515, in the town's old quarter of fine granite town houses.

A fortified house with its fine watch turret.

The Sainte Barbe chapel.

The creation of Roscoff's sub tropical garden came about because of the combination of an exceptional setting on the edges of the Morlaix Bay, a very mild climate and the enthusiastic passion of a local flower club. The garden boasts many southern hemisphere plants and is a feast for the eyes.

The quays sheltering the harbour.

A wave crashing over the quay during a storm.

Sea water therapy centre, fishing port, holiday resort, deep water ferry and cargo port, marine biology research centre… and home of the "Onion Johnies", famous throughout Great Britain for their bicycles and door-to-door sales: Roscoff has many attractions and claims to fame.

BATZ ISLAND

Situated within a stone's throw of Roscoff, Batz Island, once joined to the mainland, is watched over by its 43 metre-high lighthouse. The island's economy is based on fishing, early vegetable growing (fertilized with seaweed) and tourism.

Ruins of a monastery founded by Paul Aurélien, the Romanesque style Sainte-Anne chapel, once covered by sand, are reminders of the island's mysterious past.

Batz Island

Georges Delaselle Garden

The "colonial garden" was created at the beginning of the century on the island's southeasterly point by Georges Delaselle, a lover of exotic flowers. After years of neglect, it has now regained its former beauty. More than one thousand five hundred plants species, from all over the world, offer a flowered firework-like display of colour.

MORLAIX

Straddling the Léon and the Trégor, Morlaix is ideally situated at the end of the estuary which brings in the sea air at every tide. As a trading and privateers centre, it was one of Brittany's most active ports during the Ancien Régime. Several fine churches, aristocratic town houses, half-timbered and so called "skylight" houses and the fine collections of the Jacobins Museum, are all reminders of this rich past of the "Messieurs of Morlaix". Along the quay, the noble 18th century facade of the Tobacco Factory evokes another aspect of the town's heritage.

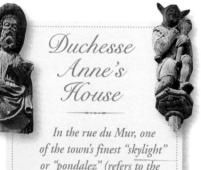

Duchesse Anne's House

In the rue du Mur, one of the town's finest "skylight" or "pondalez" (refers to the carved wooden staircases) houses is open to the public. Built in the late 15th century, it was the home of a local shipping merchant. Inside is a fine spiral staircase decorated with carved panels and religious saints.

A maritime heritage festival in the wet dock.

CALLOT ISLAND

Accessible on foot at low tide from the harbour at Carantec, Callot commands a magnificent view over the Léon and Trégor coasts of Morlaix Bay, with its collection of small islands and reefs. The spire of the 16th century Notre-Dame chapel, the site of a traditional local pilgrimage, dominates the island's sandy creeks and rocky headlands. This chapel was partly built with the island's pink granite.

If they bite you, bite them back!

The town's motto, "S'ils te mordent, mords-les !" is a play on words of the town's name dating from the 16th century. The town's privateers pillaged Bristol. In 1522, as a reprisal, the English attacked the town. To prevent a further attack, the town's wealthy merchants had the Taureau (Bull) Castle built at the entrance to Morlaix Bay.

MORLAIX BAY

On the Trégor side of Morlaix Bay is the seven thousand year old Barnenez cairn, an impressive Neolithic monument. Its layered structure covers eleven passage graves. From Pen al Lann Point in Carantec one can admire the lighthouse on the small island of Louët and the massif fortress of the Taureau (Bull) Castle. The latter, restored by Vauban and later used as a prison, was originally built in the 16th century to defend Morlaix against English attacks.

The compact mass of the Taureau (Bull) Castle.

Louët island lighthouse, built in 1860.

Barnenez Cairn.

23

On Batz Island, a carpet of armeria
spreads down into the rocky creeks.

THE PARISH CLOSES

The impressive Renaissance style belfry of Saint-Thégonnec dominates one of Brittany's most complete and finest parish closes. In a small confined space, the living and the dead are united in await of the blessed Resurrection. Nothing was to fine to express the wealth and renown of the parish, its leaders, the "fabriciens", as well as the glory of God, the Virgin Mary and the Saints. This resulted in the construction, spread over two centuries (16th c.-18th c.), of a somewhat surprising monumental ensemble in the heart of what is after all, a modest village.

SAINT-THÉGONNEC

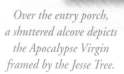

Over the entry porch, a shuttered alcove depicts the Apocalypse Virgin framed by the Jesse Tree.

The shuttered alcove of Saint-Thégonnec and the Rosary altar are the work of 17th and early 18th century artists. The style is sometimes quiet naive.

The parish closes of the Elorn Valley were the work of the Julots, merchants who had became rich in the linen and canvas trade.

In the ossuary crypt, the 1702 coloured oak carving of Saint-Sépulcre is signed Jacques Lespaignol, master carver from Morlaix.
Built in 1670, it is the work of a pupil of the famous organ builder Thomas Dallam. It was transformed by Heyer in the 19 th century and restored in 1978.

It is the latest of Brittany's great calvaries (1610) and one of the most elegant. The fine Kersanton stone has allowed the artist to work in great detail the attitude and expression of each figure, including the crowd of twisted grinning faces of Christ's torturers.

GUIMILIAU

Neighbour and thus rival to Saint-Thégonnec, the magnificence of the Guimiliau parish close is second to none. Many visitors find it more warm and welcoming because less solemn. Inside, the 1675 font is so luxuriant that it leaves one flabbergasted with admiration. The organ, built in 1690 by the Englishman Thomas Dallam, and now perfectly restored, is as renowned for its carved organ loft as it is for its stops.

Its late 16th century calvary tells the gospel story in a profusion of figures either full of life or sometimes very restrained. The Renaissance style south porch (1617) includes some medieval style scenes.

LAMPAUL-GUIMILIAU

The former "Trève" (branch) of Guimiliau had every intention of rivaling with its "mother-parish"! Mission accomplished. Massed around the foot of its fine belfry is a triumphal arch surmounted by a crucifixion, a charnel house with Doric columns and a 16th century calvary. Inside, one's attention is immediately drawn to the glory beam, finely carved with scenes from the Passion and sibyls, and the sumptuous Baroque chancel altarpieces. The Entombment (1676), carved in tuff stone, adds a solemn note to the ensemble.

PARISH CLOSES, A BRETON ART

Between the 16th and 18th centuries, competitive spirit ran high between the canvas and linen-making towns of the Elorn Valley and in this almost "holy war", embellishing their churches and closes, sometimes at great cost, was the main preoccupation for the members of the "fabrique" committee. In the closes, Breton religious art was a mix of magnificence and fantasy, majesty and naivety. A learned and popular art which expressed itself not only in the church and its different additions (triumphal arch, calvary, charnel house, sacristy, porch), but also in the furnishings and statues.

KERJEAN CASTLE

King Louis XII thought that Kerjean was worthy of him when his affairs brought him to Lower Brittany. It must be said that Renaissance Breton art reaches it high point in this magnificent home, built in the 16th century by Louis Barbier, financed with money inherited from his uncle, an abbot. The pediment portal, the chapel and its marvelous purlins, the well and its dome and lantern, the park's well; fine craftsmanship is everywhere, inspired by handbooks by Philibert Delorme and Androuet du Cerceau.

The Renaissance well.

BODILIS

On the Léonard plateau, the elegant 1570 Gothic belfry of the Bodilis parish close immediately stands out. Fifteen years later, the parish council began work on the marvelous Renaissance porch, with its fine fluted columns on the outside and the equally refined carved apostles on the inside.

LA MARTYRE

The originality of the Martyre parish close is that it is integrated into the village itself. In the past, the local fairs and markets attracted large numbers of merchants and customers, trading canvas, livestock and horses. In passing, the church committee levied a tax to finance further improvements to the church. Set on the platform of the triumphal arch, the calvary throws its shadow on the baptismal porch. Death is depicted on both the ossuary, decorated with a half naked caryatid, and the porch font, decorated with the figure of Ankou armed with a spear. A reclining Virgin, carved on the porch tympanum, adds a softer note to the general theme, which in general reflects the church's teaching so obviously based on the fear of Hell.

LANDERNEAU

During the French Revolution, Landerneau almost became the capital of the Finistère. Linking the Cornouaille bank and the Léonard bank of the river, the Rohan bridge, built in 1510, is a picturesque reminder of the town's commercial past. It is one of France's two inhabited bridges.

The 1858 Saint-Houardon church, on the north bank, was built using the belfry (rehightened) and the Renaissance porch (1604) of dark Kersanton stone recovered from a former construction.

COMMANA

On the austere fringe of the Arrée Mountains stands the rather plain belfry of Commana church. Similar to that of Bodilis, the porch leads to a rich interior. The Sainte-Anne altarpiece, with its multitude of carved figures, and the canopied font, both built in 1682, are perfect examples of Breton Gothic art.

SIZUN

Visible from afar, the fine 18th century belfry of the Saint-Suliau church in Sizun, stands out against the backdrop of the Arrée Mountains. One enters the close through a monumental triumphal arch, inspired by Roman models, and often referred to as Porz ar Maro, the gate of the dead.

Constructed in the same period, the ossuary, with its apostles, normally found in the south porch, reminds us; "Memento mori", remember you must die. Inside, the late 17th century organ, built by the Englishman Thomas Dallam, has been restored to its original multi-coloured beauty. The chancel altarpieces have something theatrical about them, with their turrets and Corinthian columns. Decoration in Breton churches feared neither excessive detail nor colour.

THE ARRÉE MOUNTAINS

In the heart of the Finistère exists a region of mystery, or even evil: the Arrée Mountains. Their highest point, at Tuchenn Gador or Roc Trévézel, is only 384 metres, but their isolation, their rough hilly landscape, their sparse population, have left these hills with a rather sinister reputation.

Here, according to tradition, was one of the gates to Hell; the nighttime washerwomen (witches) held black mass; Ankou, the scythed symbol of death, reigned without pity. One can understand why the church wanted to put these bare hills and their strange unorthodox traditions under the protection of Saint Michel. The Saint Herbot chapel, a superb example of Gothic architecture, is dedicated to the protector of livestock.

Its chancel, recumbent saint, stained glass windows and calvary are all forceful proclamations of the presence of God and men in this sombre wilderness.

Saint-Michel de Brasparts chapel.

Saint-Herbot church.

IL YEUN ELEZ, *l'ingresso dell'inferno…*

Nelle paludi del monte Saint-Michel di Brasparts, molto prima che non sia stato costruito lo sbarramento di Nestavel, esisteva un'immensa torbiera: il Yeun Elez. Era l'ingresso dell' inferno. Al tramonto, il vicario parrocchiale di Brasparts vi gettava dei cani neri nei quali aveva rinchiuso i demoni cacciati dai corpi degli indemoniati. Scomparivano immediatamente, inghiottiti nelle paludi, mentre si alzavano delle fiamme strane. La terra si metteva a tremare ed il cielo si ricopriva di enormi nuvole scure.

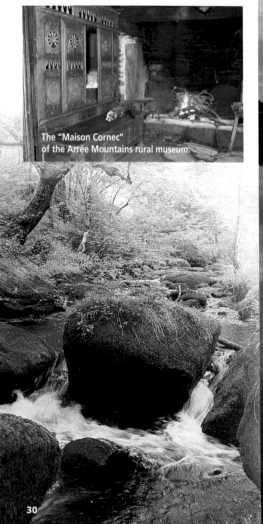

The "Maison Cornec" of the Arrée Mountains rural museum.

Huelgoat forest: a place of magic and mystery.

The village of Kerouat.

Huelgoat forest, its grottos, chasms and chaos of rocks is inevitably steeped in legend, a strange mix of King Arthur, the Dahut and Gradlon's daughter. The role of the Armorique Regional Nature Park, created in 1969, is to protect the magnificent countryside of the Arrée Mountains. Several rural museums, illustrating everyday local life, have been established in authentic local buildings (Maison Cornec at Saint-Rivoal, Kerouat mill at Commana…).

The Rusquec Manor bowl.
Was it a giant's cup?

Above: The jagged rocks of Roc Trévézel.

THE AULNE VALLEY

Between Pont-Triffen in Spézet and Port-Launay, the canalized River Aulne meanders its way between the Arrée Mountains, to the north, and the Black Mountains, to the south. Free from vehicles, a quiet towpath winds its way through a landscape more changing than you might think.

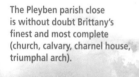

Carhaix, the Poher capital, was originally called Vorgium, the administrative centre of the Osismes during the Roman Empire period. Archaeological digs regularly bring to light evidence of this glorious past. The Senechal's (equivalent of a modern mayor during the Ancien Regime) house boasts a Renaissance style double-columned porch. Carhaix was the birthplace of Théophile Corret de la Tour d'Auvergne (1743-1800), "First Grenadier of France" and distinguished Celtic scholar.

The Châteaulin locks marked the end of the canalized part of the River Aulne.

The Pleyben parish close is splendour personified. A majestic 48 metre-high spire, a grandiose calvary on its four pillared pedestal, the exceptional size of the curious quatrefoil sacristy with its cupolas and lantern turrets. Inside, the vigour and inventiveness of the remarkable carved purlins are exceptional.

The Pleyben parish close is without doubt Brittany's finest and most complete (church, calvary, charnel house, triumphal arch).

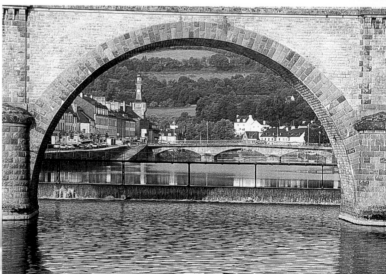

In the heart of Châteaulin, the canalized River Aulne, a salmon fisherman's paradise.

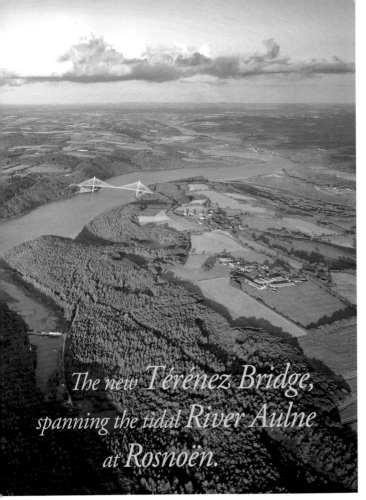

The new Térénez Bridge, spanning the tidal River Aulne at Rosnoën.

Situated on the north side of Laz forest, Trévarez Castle was built in the late 19th century by a Finistérian politician who had aspirations to become President of the Republic. He never became President but did manage to finish his costly neo-Gothic/Renaissance/Sologne castle-styled folly in the heart of the Breton moors. In 1978 the building and grounds were bought by the Conseil Général (elected County Council), renovated and opened to the public.

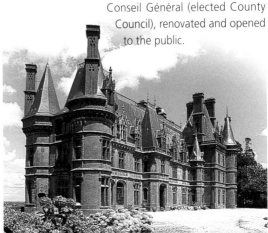

At Port-Launay, a former coastal trading port, the river becomes tidal. Downstream, the tide has an invigorating effect on the countryside around Rosnoën.

Towpath along the canalized River Aulne.

Opened in April 2011, the new Térénez Bridge, with its modern and delicate architecture, spans the tidal fjord-like part of the River Aulne. The "Breton Millau Viaduct" is the first curved cable-stayed bridge in France with a total length of 515 m with a central span of 285 m. It is without doubt a masterpiece of both technology and aesthetics.

On the inner part of the Brest roadstead, the former harbour of Le Faou has conserved reminders of its prosperous past, in the elegant church, built with Kersanton and Logonna stone and containing fine statues and altarpieces. The stone corbelled houses in the main street are an eloquent reminder of the art of living in Lower Brittany before the Revolution.

Faou church on the Brest roadstead.

FROM THE RIVER AULNE TO CROZON

Landévennec Abbey has defied the centuries. It almost disappeared during the Revolution when the last monks were dispersed. Since its foundation by Saint Guénolé in the year 500, there had been a continual religious presence. And then, in 1951, the Benedictine monks returned. New monastery buildings were constructed, including the sober but elegant Abbey, consecrated in 1965. It is an important part of Brittany's spiritual heritage, a research and study centre for Breton history, and a welcoming retreat. Landévennec has a special place in Breton hearts.

The ruins of the Romanesque abbey.

As always, the site was not chosen by accident. The monks settled near a spring, at the confluent of the Rivers Faou and Aulne and well inland on the Brest roadstead. This situation offered isolation, beauty… and fresh water. The only remains of the Romanesque abbey are some majestic 9th-12th century ruins. Just beside, the abbey museum, retracing the history of the monastic movement in Brittany, adds insight to the visit. A stone's throw from the monastery, in a bend of the River Aulne, Penforn creek, the French Navy's ships graveyard, is a rather incongruous vision in this otherwise attractive landscape. Since 1965, the Naval School is based in Lanvéoc, on the wild cliffs of the northern side of the Crozon peninsula. Just opposite, l'Île Longue is France's nuclear submarine base.

Romanesque capital.

The bare slopes of the Menez Hom.

The Menez Hom is only 330 metres high, but the beauty of this last bastion of the Black Mountains stands proud above the surrounding countryside. To the north is the tidal part of the Aulne Valley and the Brest roadstead, and to the west, Douarnenez Bay and the Crozon peninsula. It is a windswept kingdom of scarce heath land, the setting of bygone Celtic and Roman cults.

At the foot of the sacred mountain, the half Gothic, half Renaissance Sainte-Marie chapel contains some sumptuous Baroque altarpieces.

Roscanvel cliffs covered with flowering heather.

Visitors from Brest landing at Le Fret harbour in about 1930.

Crozon town centre.

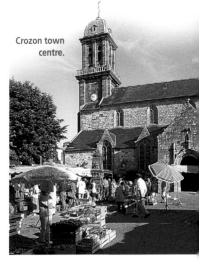

Capucins Fort

The small island on the Capucins headland was due to be fortified by Vauban in 1694, but the project was not undertaken until 1850. The gun platform was built facing the sea and the living quarters were linked to the mainland by a single-arched stone bridge. Another gun position was built facing the roadstead in 1888.

THE CROZON PENINSULA

Morgat beach.

Morgat Bay.

Camaret, Pen-hir Point.

Pen-Hat at Camaret.

The Morgat Grottos

On each side of Morgat beach the sea has eroded the cliffs cracks and gullies into superb grottos, accessible on foot at low tide, or by boat. The most beautiful is the 10 metre-high Autel (Altar) Grotto, with its colourful walls. One can easily imagine the central rock being used as an altar is some strange past ceremonies.

The Crozon peninsula is both wild and spectacular. From the cliffs of the Chèvre headland, to the mass of the Tas de Pois Rocks, standing isolated in front of Penhir Point and the strange ruin like forms of the "castle" at Dinan Point, everywhere, the grandiose and picturesque compete.

Between the headlands are fine big beaches or small pocket-sized solitary creeks. Geology lovers will find interest in the Maison des Mineraux, managed by the Armorique Park Authority. In 1880, Armand Peugeot built several villas in what was to become the town of Morgat. It has preserved to this day that refined seaside resort atmosphere.

From Espagnols Point there is a stunning view of the port and town of Brest and the "goulet", the channel at the entrance of the roadstead.

Flowered-decked village on Chèvre Point.

CAMARET

If Crozon was the peninsula's commercial centre, Camaret was it's gateway to the rest of the world. In the shadow of the chapel of Notre-Dame de Rocamadour, an important place of pilgrimage since the Middle Ages, and the Vauban Tower, built in 1689 to defend Brest against the English, one can imagine the bygone period when Camaret was an important spiny lobster fishing port.

Picture of Camaret at the beginning of the century.

The prehistoric Lagadjar lines in the morning mist. On the heath land above Camaret stand 84 standing stones in three lines, intersecting at right angles. They seem to have some connection with astronomy.

The colourful house-fronts along the quay.

The abandoned hull of a fishing boat near the Chapel of Notre-Dame de Rocamadour and the Vauban Tower.

Notre-Dame di Rocamadour

Saint Virgin,
noble patron
O lady
of Rocamadour…
Guide and comfort
in the storm
The fisherman's
frail boat;
Bring it
back to the shore
Across the
raging waters.

(approximate translation)

Because of the fertility virtues attributed to the tomb of Saint Ronan, a magnificent 15th century work in Kersanton stone, the church soon became especially venerated. In 1505, the Duchess and Queen of France, Anne of Brittany, came here to pray, in the hope of giving Louis XII a male heir.

The central square, the Saint-Ronan church and the Pénity chapel.

LOCRONAN

La Troménie.

Locronan is situated half way up a hill overlooking Douarnenez Bay. Around its central square, unique in Brittany, is a church dedicated to Saint Ronan, an ordinary bishop from Ireland, and a collection of finely built 17th and 18th century granite town houses. Every six years, vast crowds of worshipers gather for the Grande Troménie (local religious procession), a ten kilometre procession around the village, following the parish's banners. Throughout the procession, followers pay tribute to their local saints, statues of which are protected from the sun in small huts made of branches. They also go to pray at the chapel of Notre-Dame-de-Bonne-Nouvelle, with its monumental fountain.

The prosperity of Locronan developed around the growing of hemp and flax and weaving of sailcloth, so much appreciated by the French Navy, the India Company and several foreign navies. The surrounding countryside once echoed to the sound of clicking looms.

The hut of Saint Mathurin is set in the town centre and is one of the 42 stations along the circuit. Using a bell, a guardian announces the Saint and praises his or hers merits. The pilgrims then leave a small offering in a copper dish. Saint Mathurin heels depression and folly and saves souls from Purgatory.

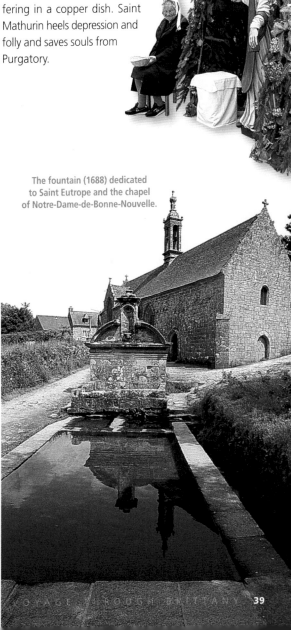

The fountain (1688) dedicated to Saint Eutrope and the chapel of Notre-Dame-de-Bonne-Nouvelle.

DOUARNENEZ

Nestled in the curve of its bay, Douarnenez has always lived from fishing. At the beginning of the century, hundreds of sailing boats fished sardines, a livelihood not only for the fishermen, but also the employees of the local the canning factories. Sail has now been replaced by modern deep-sea and coastal trawlers.

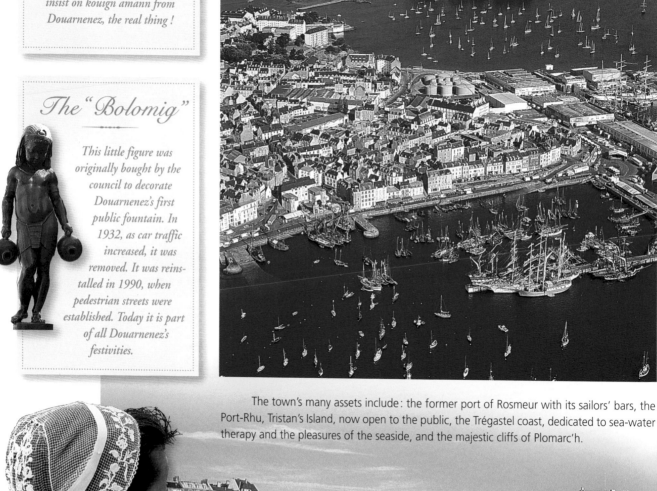

The town's many assets include: the former port of Rosmeur with its sailors' bars, the Port-Rhu, Tristan's Island, now open to the public, the Trégastel coast, dedicated to sea-water therapy and the pleasures of the seaside, and the majestic cliffs of Plomarc'h.

Sainte Anne - The Bretons Grandmother

Since way back in time, the mother of the Virgin Mary has been honoured at Saint-Anne-la-Palud. Local tradition claims that the origins of the "pardon" (annual local procession) go back as far as the legend of the town of Ys. The present day chapel, in neo-Gothic style, houses a very moving statue of Sainte Anne and Mary in coloured stone.

Along Douarnenez Bay, the vast beaches of Pentrez, Lestrevet and Porz ar Vag.

With its Boat Museum and wet dock, the Port Rhu estuary has become a Mecca of maritime heritage. Exhibitions and displays include many types of boats, fishing techniques, life on board and many other aspects of sea-related activities.

TRÉBOUL
Saint-Jean chapel

Near the strand, the Saint-Jean chapel (extensively rebuilt in 1746) has modern and lively stained glass windows designed in 1986 by René Quéré, a local artist.

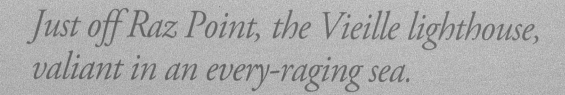

Just off Raz Point, the Vieille lighthouse, valiant in an every-raging sea.

CAP SIZUN

az Point, this majestic granite spur, destined to a never-ending battle with the sea, has been carefully rehabilitated. With the eyesores of the past gone, one can appreciated the stunning face to face contest between rock and water. The criss-cross beams of several lighthouses mark out the surrounding waters. Out at sea, the island of Sein seems so fragile in the heart of such a tempestuous nature.

Notre-Dame des Naufragés
(Our Lady of the Shipwrecked).

The Vieille lighthouse.

RAZ POINT

Van Point has a different kind of majesty. The steep and jagged cliffs are as equally impressive but the atmosphere is more serene.

Perhaps this is because the Saint They chapel, invoked by seamen in distress, has, in its modest way, kept watch on the cliff edge since the 16th century? In days of old, the Baie des Trépassés (Bay of the Dead) was the starting point for the ultimate journey towards the island of Avalon, the Celts Paradise.

Cap-Sizun Headdress

Although more discreet than its Bigouden neighbour, the kapenn headdress nevertheless displays a certain elegance combined with a touch of humour.

AUDIERNE

Boats from Audierne fish for the more profitable species, including spiny lobster, sea perch, devilfish, turbot and skate. Beside the busy quays and the Poulgoazec fish market, the River Goyen opens out into a fine sinuous estuary.

SEIN ISLAND

Some two hundred and fifty inhabitants still hang on to raft-like island of Sein. With an average height above the sea of only 1.5 metres, and surrounded by numerous reefs, the island has always been at the mercy of the elements. The new 1952, 48 metres-high lighthouse, with a range of thirty nautical miles, adds a little reassurance. The Free French Memorial at Quillivic is a reminder that in June 1940, 130 of the island's men put to sea to join General de Gaulle in England.

The playful ballet of dolphins contrasts with the severe immobility of the Sein island's lighthouse.

Along the harbour quay, tightly packed houses.

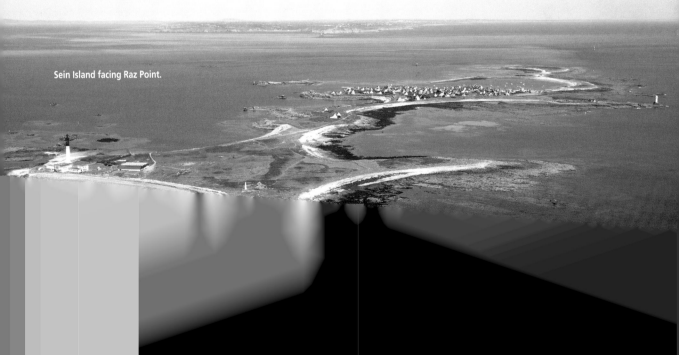

Sein Island facing Raz Point.

THE BIGOUDEN PAYS

Here is a peninsula washed by the sea and the River Odet with its four fishing ports, bringing in daily fresh catches: Le Guilvinec, capital of the maritime sector, Loctudy, Saint-Guénolé and Lesconil. Among the fifty or so species fished, two are emblematic, live prawns and devilfish. These are landed every day between 5 and 6 o'clock in the afternoon and immediately sold by auction in the fish market.

Prawn fishing boats and trawlers at quay in Loctudy.

Three headdresses defy time... and the wind!

L'Ile Tudy. In the 5th century, Saint Tudy, arriving from Ireland, established a hermitage on what was then a deserted island.

Do not miss the trawlers returning to port! It is the Bigouden region's symbol of their dependence of the sea, fishing and the numerous associated activities. In the 16th century Penmarc'h had one of Europe's largest fleets. Its ships transported wine from Bordeaux and Toulouse pastel (used for dyestuffs) to Flanders and England. Towards 1590, international competition and the wars of religion brought this prosperity to an end. But the souvenir of this glorious period is still present, particularly in the carved sailing ships found in the churches. The Joie chapel, also a reminder of past glory, stills salutes the fishermen when then return to port.

40 fishing boats returning to Guilvinec, every evening, is a delight for the numerous visitors.

On a hill, overlooking Audierne Bay, is the moving Tronoën calvary. The figures, aged by rain, sea air and salt, have a heart-touching humanity emanating from them. Carved in about 1460, mainly in course grained granite, the scenes depict the main episodes of the Childhood and Passion of Christ. The bare-breasted reclining Virgin, carved in Kersanton stone, has undeniable beauty. The chapel, built at the same time, marks the harmonious landscape with its powerful silhouette.

Mary, with her generous and naked bossom, is resting. Strangely, the child at the foot of the bed is between 10 and 12 years old and seems to be pointing to its mother.

The Bigouden headdress has never ceased to become taller since the beginning of the century. Today, at 33 centimetres, it is defies both the wind and restrictions of modern lifestyle. In common with those from Plougastel-Daoulas, the Bigouden women are the last of Brittany's women to remain faithful to their traditional dress. In a few years, the page will be turned.

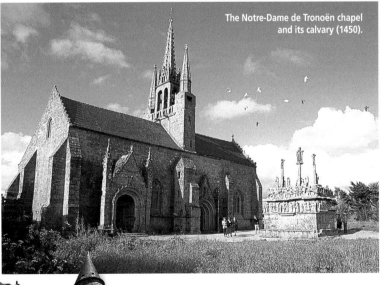

The Notre-Dame de Tronoën chapel and its calvary (1450).

The Bigouden capital has conserved three monuments which summaries its past. The feudal castle, now houses the town hall and the Bigouden Museum. The Pères Carmes church has elegant Gothic architecture. In 1675, the 13th and 14th century Lambour church had its belfry decapitated by the King's troops in reprisal to the Bonnets Rouges (Red Caps) revolt.

The Embroiderers

The Bigouden have always been renowned as "leveurs de fil", embroiderers. The men worked on the shirt fronts and waistcoats, and the women on the headdresses and fine ceremonial dress. The designs differed depending on the wealth and status of the customer. The sun represented joy; the heart love; a ram's horn force; a saw tooth work…

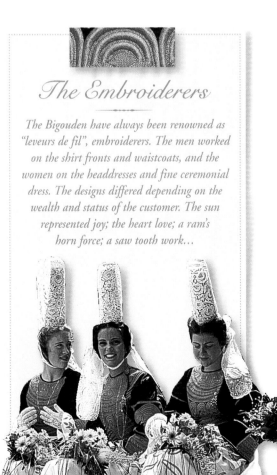

QUIMPER

Built between the 13th and 15th centuries, and placed under the protection of Saint Corentin, the Gothic cathedral has recently undergone extensive renovation. The stonework, paintings and stained glass windows have all recovered their original splendour.

Corbelled turret overlooking the River Steir.

Saint Jean Discalcéat "Santig Du" 1278-1349.

Behind the chancel, the statue of the Santig Du is particularly venerated. This monk from Quimper devoted much of his life to his fellow parishioners during the epidemics of the Middle Ages. Flanked by corbelled half-timbered houses, the rue Kéréon (cobblers, in Breton) offers an stunning view of cathedral.

In the old quarters, the place au Beurre and Terre-au-Duc, home of the former nobles and bourgeoisie, half-timbered and stone-built house alternate. With the River Odet crossing the town, the charming wooded slopes of Mont Frugy, the Cornouaille capital has managed to preserve its natural assets. According to legend, the town was founded by King Gradlon, after he escaped from the town of Ys when it was flooded.

Rue Kéréon and Saint Corentin cathedral.

La place au Beurre (Butter Square).

Three museums are guardians of the town's artistic reputation. The Fine Arts Museum, with its works of the Pont-Aven group of artists; the Breton Museum, dedicated to popular tradition (superb collections of headdresses and tradition dress); the Faïence (earthenware) Museum, pays homage to three centuries of local know-how.

La place Terre-au-Duc.

THE RIVER ODET

For fifteen kilometres, between Quimper and Bénodet, the River Odet meanders, widening and narrowing again between its steep wooded banks.

Old fashioned houses and their gardens add a certain distinguished touch to the scenery. In some places, only turrets are visible amongst the foliage. In others, like Kerouzien, the manor house stands proud for all to see. The Bishops of Quimper chose Lanniron, on the river, as their summer residence.

More recently, Eric Tabarly and his Pen-Duick dropped anchor here, on the banks at Gousenac'h.

From the Cornouaille Bridge situated just before the estuary, linking the Bigouden and Fouesnant pays, there is a superb view of Bénodet and Sainte-Marine.

The Odet estuary.

Kerouzien Castle on the River Odet.

BÉNODET

The lighthouse and beach on the Coq headland.

Bénodet, situated on the Odet estuary, was developed as a holiday resort last century for the local Quimperois and also for British visitors. Exposed both to the river and the sea, the climate is mild, the vegetation luxuriant and the beaches sheltered. Two lighthouses marked the entrance to the estuary, the Pyramide, and the more modest Coq. The coast road between the port and the beach offers agreeable views of the busy multi-coloured estuary and the harbour and villas of Sainte-Marine on the Bigouden side. Bénodet is an ideal boarding place for the launches that operate along the Odet and Pont-l'Abbé rivers and the serve the Glénan islands.

CONCARNEAU

After Boulogne and Lorient, Concarneau is France's third fresh fish port. At the back of the bay, two worlds coexist: the ramparts of the Medieval Walled Town, an essential defensive bastion of the former Duchy and later Province of Brittany, and the ultra-modern port. If in Concarneau tuna (tropical and germon) is king, many other species are fished. These include devilfish, prawns, cod and even sardines.

With its deep-sea factory trawlers, inshore trawlers and other small fishing boats, the port is a perfect summary of the whole fishing industry.

Concarneau's seaward side offers its beaches and sea front boulevard, where one can visit the marinarium of the Marine Biology Laboratory.

In the past, local fishermen only ever fished sardines. Those times have long since gone, but their souvenir still echoes in the Walled Town, along its streets of old houses and sailors' bars and in the rich Fishing Museum.

There are a thousand and one ways of preparing tuna: grilled, oven-cooked, fried, tinned...

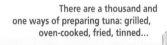

THE GLÉNAN
Islands

Fifteen kilometres from the mainland, the ten or so small islands of the Glénan archipelago, so well known in sailing circles, are clustered around "la Chambre", a closed bay of crystal clear water. One can also visit the Ile Saint-Nicolas by boat.

Port beach.

BEG-MEIL

In 1895, Marcel Proust was one of the first to appreciate the mixed maritime and countryside charm of Beg-Meil, one of Fouesnant region's seaside resorts, evoked in his Jean Santeuil.

The writer particularly liked the orchards growing right down to the sea. Since then, Beg-Meil has lost non of its charm. Its little harbour, its beaches, its rocks, its trees and its discreet but impressive water-side villas, all make it a resort much sought after by those who love authenticity and a certain *art de vivre*.

PORT-LA-FORÊT

In a hollow of the Forêt Bay, flanked by a golf course and Kerleven beach, Port-La-Forêt is a shelter for hundreds of pleasure-craft. Protected from offshore winds by the Cap Coz, the weather is extremely mild.

All around, the countryside of the pays of Fouesnant, has preserved its dense wooded character, with picturesque paths leading directly onto the beaches.

PONT-AVEN

The painter Paul Gaugin made Pont-Aven famous. His stays in the "town of mills" from 1886 onwards, his meeting with Émile Bernard, gave birth to the Pont-Aven School, considered as pioneers of modern art. The Municipal Museum, many art galleries, the Yellow Christ in the fine Gothic chapel of Trémalo, which inspired Gaugin, the Bois d'Amour, all pay homage to this glorious period of the town's history. The harbour on the inner estuary, once a small trading port, and the Xavier Grall Promenade (named after the magnificent and sometimes dramatic Breton poet), show two contrasting sides of the River Aven.

Traou Mad galettes (Butter biscuits)

"Made with fine Breton butter, and cooked in the oven", said the advertisement of Mr. Le Vilain, maker of the famous "Traou Mad" biscuits. Since the 1950's, these biscuits have become very popular. Biscuit manufacturers far and wide, now use the name of the town of painters… and gastronomes.

At nightfall, the mills add magic to the Aven. Coasters no longer come up the river but the harbour has lost none of its charm.

FROM TRÉVIGNON TO LE POULDU

The south-east coast of the Cornouaille region is a succession of flower-decked cliffs, creeks of fine sand and invigorating and secret estuaries. The countryside hides small villages of tastefully renovated thatched cottages, such as Kerascoët in Névez, and chapels housing venerable statues, as in Notre-Dame-de-la Clarté at Trémorvézen, or the pretty sanctuary of Saint-Philibert in Moëlan-sur-Mer.

The small harbour of Doëlan in Clohars-Carnoët.

The Notre-Dame-de-la-Clarté chapel, in the form of a Latin cross, is also called Chapelle-des-trois-Marie.

Meandering between wooded banks, the rivers Aven, Belon and Laïta, which separate the Finistère from the Morbihan, bring the tonic sea air to the quiet inland countryside areas. Small scale pot or net fishing is carried out on the miniature estuaries of Brigneau, Merrien and Doëlan.

Since the beginning of the century, Port-Manech, Kerfany-les-Pins and Le Pouldu, have been popular but human-sized resorts. From 1889 onwards, at le Pouldu, it was Gaugin and some of his friends who came, long before holiday makers, in an attempt to get away from the noisy "crowds" of Pont-Aven.

As a change from the invigorating sea air, nothing is better than a stroll through Carnoët forest, along the banks of the Laïta.

Grands Sables beach in Le Pouldu.

Bélon Oysters

The rearing of flat oysters in the river at Bélon dates from 1864. Because of its delicious hazelnut taste and a mixture of salt and fresh water, the "bélon" soon became renowned. Today, although the rearing of seed oyster and some stages of growing are carried out elsewhere, the final stages of rearing are still the exclusivity of the Bélon oyster beds.

Côtes-d'Armor
A VOYAGE THROUGH BRITTANY

Two former bishoprics, Tréguier and Saint-Brieuc, a multitude of "pays" (Goëlo, Poudouvre, Mené…), a superb coastline (cliffs at Fréhel and Plouha, Jaudy and Trieux estuaries), old towns with paved streets full of history (Dinan, Tréguier, Moncontour), the island of Bréhat, with its luxuriant southern vegetation: are only some of the reasons to want to discover the Côtes d'Armor! The region that gave birth to Saint Yves (1253-1303), the patron saint of Brittany, is also the home of the Pleumeur-Bodou Telecommunications Centre, with its famous dome, a symbol of Breton innovation.

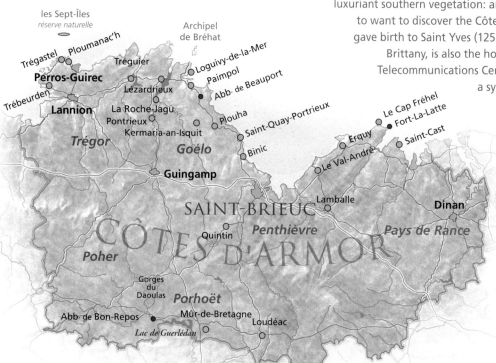

Le "Père Trébeurden".

LANNION

Lannion is the capital of a region where megalithic standing stones and satellites exist side by side. At Pleumeur-Bodou, the Telecommunications Museum and the Planetarium, projecting the visitor resolutely forward into future technology, is a neighbour of the 4.500 year old christianized standing stone of Saint-Uzec. Bathed by the waters of the River Léguer, Lannion has its "inspired hill", the heights of Brélévenez (Mount of Joy in French), reached by the 143 steps of the majestic Trinité stairway.

Founded, it is said, by a military order, the Romanesque and Gothic style church contains many fine altarpieces and, in the crypt, a superb 18th century polychrome stone Entombment.

Place du Général Leclerc, the walls of the half-timbered, corbelled houses are decorated with caryatids.

The Brélévenez steps.

GUINGAMP

In Guingamp the majestic silhouette of the 14th century Gothic basilica of Notre-Dame is imposing. Inside, the multitude of pillars creates an atmosphere of mystery. The feeling is similar on the place du Centre, in front of the mermaids and the fanciful elegance of the La Plomée fountain (18th c.).

TRÉGUIER

Overlooking the Jaudy Valley, Tréguier, a bishopric until the French Revolution, is a small town where the Breton soul and spirituality are deeply rooted.

The Saint Tugdual Gothic cathedral, built in the 14th and 15th centuries, incorporated a Romanesque Hasting tower. The People's Porch rose-window and the delicate lines of the nave's pillars and arches are but two examples of the building's overall majesty and elegance.

The house of Ernest Renan, now a museum.

Saint Yves, patron saint of lawyers

In 1253, Tréguier was the birthplace of Yves Helory de Kermartin, priest and defender of the poor and humble. He was canonized in 1347. On the 19th of May each year, the Saint Yves pardon is an occasion for men of law to meet for a grand mess in the cathedral and a procession to saint's native village of Minihy.

The cloister is a gem of the Flamboyant Gothic style, and an ideal place to meditate on the works of Ernest Renan (1823-1892), a local writer, often misunderstood during his lifetime. His house is open to the public. Dominated by two square towers, the port on the River Jaudy reminders us that this quiet episcopal town is an active trading gateway to the open sea.

The port and the cathedral.

*On the Ploumanac'h headland,
the Men-Ruz (red stone) lighthouse
dominates the granite rocks.*

THE PINK GRANITE COAST

Bottle Rock.

Between Perros-Guirec and Trébeurden, the coast has been subject to such geological upheaval that it has been turned upside down… and become extremely beautiful. The name of "pink granite coast" in fact covers a whole range of rocks and colours, from course-grained pink to fine-grained orange-beige. In an infinite variety of boulders or jagged cliffs, the coast is a mass of small islands and folds, an amazing and diversified collection of beauty spots. Heaps of apparently unstable boulders with evocative shapes, sometimes surrounded by a multi-coloured heathland, are one of Brittany's most unique and somewhat magic landscapes. At Ploumanac'h, in order to round the headland, the coastal footpath meanders its way through a chaos of creeks and boulders. In the middle of the bay, on Costaéres island, is the strange larger than life silhouette of the neo-Medieval castle built by a Polish engineer in the late 19th century. Here he was host to his friend and compatriot, Henryk Sienkiewicz, the author of *Quo Vadis*.

Costaéres Castle.

Saint Guirec and young eligable women

On the beach of Ploumanac'h, the small oratory of Saint Guirec is surrounded by water. According to an ancient tradition, young women in search of a husband would come to stick a pin into Saint Guirec's nose. If the pin stayed in, they were sure to marry within the year. If not, they had to wait another year. Today, a granite statue has replaced the old mouldy wax saint, and young women interogate the statue in vain.

Sant C'Hireg is the Breton name of Ploumanac'h's venerated Saint Guirec. This cutter is a excellent modern replica of a Camaret spiny lobster fishing boat in the time of sail.

Trestraou beach at Perros-Guirec.

From Coz Pors beach to the Grève Blanche and all around the island of Renote (now joined to the mainland), the coastal footpath winds its way through a multitude of granite boulders offering a endless variety of views. What a contrast there is between the placid coves and geological upheavals that gave rise to the strange and sometimes tortured shapes of the rocks!

From 1866 onwards the charms of Perros-Guirec as a resort attracted its first holiday makers. At the beginning of the century, its sea front boulevards, its footpaths, its beaches of Trestrignel and Trestraou, the Romanesque and Gothic Saint-Jacques church, were much appreciated by two famous local residents, the writer Charles Le Goffic and the painter Maurice Denis. Since then, the wet dock of the important pleasure-craft harbour has been created in a sheltered setting on the inner bay.

Trégastel, leaving Coz Pors in front of the "Dice Rock".

The Seven Islands Nature Reserve

Out to sea from Ploumanac'h, the small uninhabited Seven Islands archipelago covers hardly more than forty hectares at high tide, but since 1912 it is Brittany's most important ornithological site. Managed by the Ligue pour la Protection des oiseaux (bird protection association), the nature reserve is France's most important nesting site for seabirds. Gannets and several types of puffins established here are in constant peril of their mortal enemy, oil pollution. Launches, operating from Trestraou beach in Perros-Guirec, take visitors to Moines Island, the only one accessible to the public.

PAIMPOL

ontrary to what is suggested in the "Paimpolaise", the famous song (1895) written by Théodore Botrel, there are hardly any cliffs in Paimpol. There is just a wide bay, peppered with reefs and small islands. During the Middle Ages, on one of the islands, Saint-Riom, a monastery existed. A few kilometres to the north, at Arcouest Point, boarding place for the island of Bréhat, there is a splendid view of whole jagged coast.

In Paimpol, the saga of its cod fishing past is present everywhere. The Musée de la Mer recalls and illustrates the past's Icelandic fishing expeditions. The houses along the Morand Quay are those of former ship owners. The statue of Notre-Dame-de-Bonne-Nouvelle, on show in the church, is paraded every year during the "Icelanders" pardon. This epic past, still alive and strong, has pride of place in local memory.

Old-fashioned sailing ships in the wet dock.

PLOUBAZLANEC

aimpol's small neighbouring port paid a heavy tribute to fishing in the Icelandic waters. In the cemetery, a moving "wall of the departed" pays homage to all those sailors lost at sea or struck down by illness. At the *Croix des veuves* (the widows' cross), fishermens wives would watch out for the returning schooners.

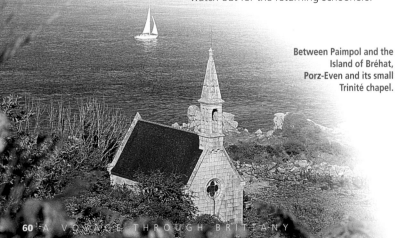

Between Paimpol and the Island of Bréhat, Porz-Even and its small Trinité chapel.

Icelandic Fishermen

The last cod fishing campaign to Icelandic waters was in 1935. This epic period began in 1852 when the Paimpol fishermen decided to abandon the Newfoundland fishing grounds and head further north.

Its peak was in 1895, when the port's fleet numbered eighty schooners. These epic, hard and dangerous six-month campaigns, often fatal for both sailors and deckhands, were immortalized in Pierre Loti's "Pêcheur d'Islande" (1886).

LOGUIVY-DE-LA-MER

A charming song by François Budet has added to the notoriety of this discreet little port on the Trieux estuary. Previous to this song, many famous people have succumbed to the charm of its quays heaped with lobster pots. These included the painter Henri Rivière, Charles Menne and Mathurin Méheut, Pierre Loti and even Lenin. The boats fished edible crab and spiny lobster. *"Loguivy-de-la-Mer, in the back of your old harbour, the carcasses of boats already dead are piled up".*

Early morning start to a fishing trip in Loguivy-de-la-Mer.

PONTRIEUX

On the main square in Pontrieux, the half-timbered corbelled so-called "Eiffel Tower" house was probably built in the 16th century by a rich merchant. The position of the town on the inner estuary meant it could be reached by sail coasters who came to load cereals and sailcloth.

Roche-Jagu Castle in Ploëzal.

A few kilometres to the north, situated in a grandiose setting on a bend of the River Trieux, is the Roche-Jagu Castle with its impressive 15th century walls and ornately carved chimneys. It is owned by the département and use for exhibitions and displays.

The rugged coastline at Château Point near Plougrescant.

Saint-Gonéry chapel (15th-17th c.)

At the entrance to Plougrescant, with its curiously leaning wooden and lead belfry and its outside pulpit, is the Romanesque and Gothic style Saint-Gonéry chapel. On the nave's wooden panels are late 15th century paintings, in a rather touchingly naiv style, depicting the lives of Adam and Eve and other stories from the Old and New Testaments.

Saint-Michel chapel.

The Men-Joliguet beacon.

Port-Clos.

Kervillon

Le Rosedo

Le Birlot

Ile Grou Ezen

Crec'h Simo

Ile Biniguet

Ile Raguénès

Port-Clos creek.

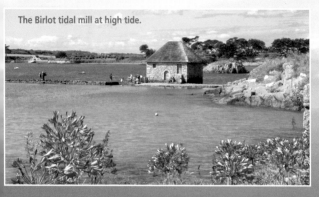

The Birlot tidal mill at high tide.

The Paon lighthouse.

Pointe du Paon

Ile ar-Morbic

Ile Séhéres

La Corderie

Ile Lavrec

Ile Logodec

Ile de Bréhat

La Chambre

Le Gerzido

Port-Clos

Crec'h Guen

Le Goaréva

THE BRÉHAT ARCHIPELAGO

Ravishingly beautiful. The north coast's paradise. Writers and painters, including Foujitd and Matisse (who came here to find inspiration), have all sung the praises of the "island of flowers", set in the midst of an archipelago of an unbelievable number of small scattered islands and reefs. Joined by a bridge are two islands, the south island, more inhabited, and the north island, more wild. With no cars, a luxuriant vegetation, the presence of many birds and an infinite variety of beauty spots, every step on the island is shear poetry. One is overcome with a feeling of peace and tranquillity in the small bays and creeks. In the evening, when all the lighthouses on the island and in the surrounding sea are ablaze, it is total magic.

BEAUPORT ABBEY

Sheltered in Paimpol bay, in a superb setting of water, strand and greenery, the romantic ruins of Beauport Abbey are now under the watchful protection of the "Conservatoire du Littoral" (a national body in charge of France's coastal heritage). The principle parts of the edifice were built in the mid 13th century by Premonstratensian monks. At the time, it was considered to be Brittany's finest and most important abbey.

During the French Revolution it was used as a gunpowder factory, but the fine Norman style chapter house was saved from destruction.

One can visit the rooms of the chaplaincy, the press-house, the grand cellar, the guest-house and the refectory. Looking directly at the sky, the arches and windows seem to purvey a somewhat gloomy poetic atmosphere, in keeping with the placid bay and the surrounding ponds.

The Macabre Dance of Kermaria-an-Isquit

On the walls of the nave of Kermaria chapel in Plouha is a rather disturbing 15th century fresco depicting the Macabre Dance. The king and the bishop, the knight and the merchant, the ploughman and the hermit, are all carried away in a fatal dance.

PLOUHA

Plouha cliffs, Brittany's highest, stretch along fifteen kilometres of coast, reaching a maximum height of 104 m at Plouha Point. Along the Gwin Zégal coastal footpath one discovers a coastal landscape of striking beauty.

Above Cochat Bay is a commemorative stele in memory of the resistance network that helped 135 allied pilots return to England in November 1943. The operation's code name was Bonaparte, thus the name of the beach.

Bonaparte beach.

SAINT-QUAY-PORTRIEUX

The fashion of sea bathing began in Saint-Quay in 1841 ! Even a community of local nuns took to the waters. The resort developed and now has many assets: several beaches of fine sand, a thousand berth marina and a ferry terminal.

Saint-Quay-Portrieux's fishing and pleasure-craft ports.

Fishermen from Portrieux and Binic are believed to have started cod fishing around Newfoundland in 1612. At its peak in the 19th century the Newfoundland fleet was made up of schooners of 150 to 300 tons, manned by a total of 2 800 crew. Both ports have now turned to fishing mackerel, bass, scallop and crustaceans.

Panoramic view of Binic harbour.

BINIC

On Binic's quays one can still sense the port's glorious past when more than fifty ships and 1.500 crew went fishing for cod in the Newfoundland waters.

Banche beach in Binic.

Several 17th century ship-owners houses and the Cheval Blanc auberge are reminders of this glorious past. Tourism is now the main activity, with its marina and the two well sheltered Blanche and Goulet beaches.

The old quarters

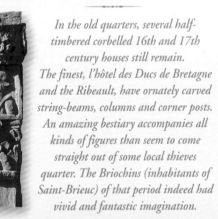

In the old quarters, several half-timbered corbelled 16th and 17th century houses still remain. The finest, l'hôtel des Ducs de Bretagne and the Ribeault, have ornately carved string-beams, columns and corner posts. An amazing bestiary accompanies all kinds of figures than seem to come straight out of some local thieves quarter. The Briochins (inhabitants of Saint-Brieuc) of that period indeed had vivid and fantastic imagination.

Saint-Brieuc is first and foremost a vast bay, renowned for is scallops, its mussel rearing (on bouchots, wooden posts stuck in the sand), and its vast numbers of seabirds. During the big spring tides the sea retreats seven kilometres ! The town of Saint-Brieuc is situated in a rather odd position above the River Gouët, which then deepens just before the estuary at the harbour at Légué.

The town's symbol, the fortress-like cathedral, is indeed both plain and impressive. Its two 14th and 15th century towers have simple plain walls surmounted by machicolations, but inside the remarkable Baroque styled Annunciation altarpiece is an explosion of festoons and gold decorations.

The Annunciation altarpiece.

QUINTIN

The atmosphere in Quintin is that of an old somewhat sleepy provincial town behind the majestic fronts of its 18 th century town-houses. Gone are the times when sailcloth insured the town's fame and prosperity, when local nobility flouted the civil and religious authorities by ostentatiously displaying their Huguenot faith, when the town's population was larger than that of Saint-Brieuc.

Near a 17 th century pavilion (part of a more ambitious project which was never finished), the Louis XV logis of the castle is a visit, for its collection of rare and precious objects and the refined exhibitions held there.

LAMBALLE
"The Executioner's House"

The 17 th century "Executioner's House" is so named because it is situated on the place de Martray, where, in former times, local justice was administered. This fine Medieval corbelled half-timbered dwelling now houses the Mathurin Méheut (1882-1958) Museum. Born in Lamballe, he painted scenes of everyday Breton life in a warm vivid style.

LE VAL-ANDRÉ

Since 1882, Le Val André and its execeptional beach, one of the north coast's finest, has been a delight for all lovers of the sea.

The beach is backed by the Pléneuf headland with its view extending from Saint-Brieuc Bay to Cap Erquay. Opposite is the bird sanctuary of the small island of Verdelet, home of terns, seagulls and shags.

Around the Grande Guette headland, the GR34 (coastal footpath) leads down to the Flora estuary, sheltering the charming little harbour of Dahouët. For centuries its boats fished Newfounland and Icelandic waters, but now its main activity is scallop harvesting.

Dahouët is the home port of the old rigger La Pauline , a decked lugger with elegant sails. This boat is a faithful replica of a traditional lugger, built by a group of marine heritage enthusiasts. Offering trips to sea, on board everyone can have a taste of old tradiotional sailing methods.

La Pauline

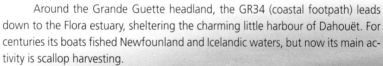

ERQUY

Cap Erquy a is superb natural area. It offers seven beaches, either in the heart of the resort or isolated along the well preserved coast, an active fishing port and archaeological remains, reminders of great moments from the past. Erquy's charm is that it is everything but an ordinary seaside resort.

Fishing in Erquy

At the foot of a cliff, marked by its small lighthouse, Erquy harbour is both picturesque and active. Its fishing fleet counts a hundred boats. Its speciality, for which it is renown throughout France, is the collection of scallops and clams. To avoid over exploitation of the resources, the activity is strictly reglulated. The season is from November to April, two hours a day, and only four days a week. During the summer the boats fish sole, hake and skate. The scallop fishing boats are anchored alongside the "Sainte-Jeanne", a modern copy of a traditional sixteen-metre sailing boat.

Along the coastal footpath one can see the Catuélan and Pleine-Garenne Ditches, built by the Celtic Cariosolite tribe before the arrival of the Romans. One can also admire the 17th century coalnut ovens, the Lourtuais fountain, the heather covered cliffs, the masses of screeching seabirds amongst the rocks, isolated Robinson Crusoe-like beaches and many different beautiful view points.

Portuais beach situated in the cape's nature reserve.

LE CAP FRÉHEL

One will never be bored with the spectacular natural scenery of the Cap Fréhel. Its jagged cliffs of schist and pink gritstone rise seventy metres above the sea. When the wind blows across this impressive headland, the atmosphere of a never ending battle of the elements is haunting. An excellent way to discover this jagged coastline is along the GR 34 (coastal footpath).

The lighthouse, rebuilt in 1950, is beside a former 'fire-tower' built by Vauban in 1695. It was originally fueled by charcoal and later by fish oil. In spring and summer the 400 hectares of gorse and heather heathland explode with gold and purple colour. But did you know that carnivorous plants and rare gentian can also be found hidden in hollows of the most peaty areas?

The bird sanctuary

Between seven and eight hundred couples of seabirds nest on the jagged cliffs of Cap Fréhel, part of which is a bird sanctuary.
Among the species than can be seen, in an incessant aerial ballet above the cliffs, are shags, kittiwakes and fulmar petrels. Also adding to the site's renown are razorbills and guillemots, so vulnerable to marine oil pollution. With one hundred and forty pairs in 1995, the Cap Fréhel has France's most important colony of guillemots.

FORT-LA-LATTE

The keep and the ramparts of the fortress.

Could one dream of a more unsociable setting than a stronghold ? On its rock closed in by the sea, protected on the land side by two gullies, the Roche-Guyon fort, later named Fort-la-Latte, stands proud with its walls, keep and 14th and 15th century towers, seemingly defying the elements and time.

The local masters, the Goyons, lords of Matignon, had a surprising destiny. In the 18th century, Jacques de Goyon bought an impressive town house in Paris, which he named after his Breton lands. It later became the official residence of the French Prime Minister. In 1775, his son married Louise Grimaldi, daughter of the Prince of Monaco. Ever since then, the Matignon church bells ring to celebrate every royal birth on the famous rock.

If the fortress is still sometimes attacked, it is for more peaceful reasons. Such a setting was bound to inspire film directors, including Fleischer in 1957 (The Vikings) and De Broca for his film *Les Chouans.*

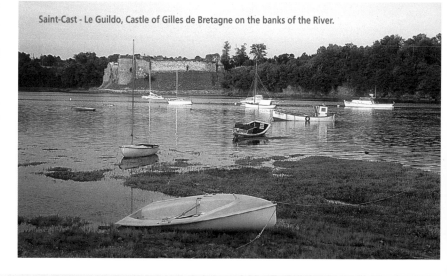

Saint-Cast - Le Guildo, Castle of Gilles de Bretagne on the banks of the River.

Bouchot mussels in Saint-Cast Bay

Mussels are reared on wooden poles called buchots, fixed into the sand in the tidal area of the bay. The spat are collected on long horizontal ropes which are then wrapped around the buchots. Mussels reach their commercial size in less than two years.

LE GUILDO

The River Arguenon widens into an estuary and joins the Channel near the ruins of feudal castle of Le Guildo. After centuries of neglect, the walls are now being patiently restored.

The setting, both romantic and a little gloomy, is still haunted by the tragic story of Gilles de Bretagne, who became the fiancé of a rich heir from Le Guildo. This son of Duke Jean V was up against the hostility of his elder brother François 1st of Brittany, who finished by having him suffocated in 1450.

The Saint-Cast-Le Guildo marina.

The main beach.

SAINT-CAST

Sheltered by a headland of the same name, the resort of Saint-Cast began to expand at the end of the last century when the area around Garde Point was developed.

Amid the pines and acacia, the villas and hotels attracted wealthy visitors who came to enjoy the charms of Arguenon Bay.

That charm still exists today, whether it be along the main beach, in the old quarter of Isle, or in Port Jacquet, where scallop fishermen and pleasure-craft owners anchor side by side. The 11th of September 1758 seems long ago, when the battle of Saint-Cast raged between the Franco-Breton and the English fleets, causing very heavy loses on both sides.

During the Ramparts Festival, riders joust in the lists.

The harbour, the old bridge and the Rance Valley.

Anne of Brittany

Among the stained glass windows of Saint-Malo church in Dinan is one, moving for all Bretons, illustrating Anne of Brittany's visit to the town in 1505. Queen of France for the second time - she was then married to Louis XII - the Duchess began a Tro Breiz, a religious pilgrimage visiting all the tombs of the founder saints of Brittany's bishoprics. At the height of her popularity she reestablished relations with her faithful subjects and prayed that she might give a male heir to her royal husband. She died nine years later, in 1514, at the age of thirty seven, her prays still unanswered.

Jerzual Gate.

DINAN

Half-timbered houses on the "place de l'Apport".

Is Dinan Brittany's most evocative old town? Its half-timbered houses, sometimes on wooden pillars, its ramparts and keep, its churches, all make up a striking example of Middle Ages architecture. The corbelled houses, somewhat askew, are crowded along the narrow streets, still in their original layout, and overlooked by the Horloge (Clock) Tower, seat of the local community during the Ancien Régime.

The Romanesque porch of the Saint-Sauveur church is alive with carvings of eel-like creatures and mermaids. The sanctuary houses the heart of Du Guesclin, a local-born knight who later became Constable of France. Going down the hill, the windy streets of Jerzual and Petit-Fort, lined with picturesque houses, were old liaison roads between the town and the harbour on the banks of the River Rance.

THE GUERLÉDAN PAYS
Mûr-de-Bretagne

The building of Guerlédan hydroelectric dam, between 1923 and 1930, created a lake in the Blavet Valley. The steep wooded and sinuous banks make an unusual landscape for Brittany. The area is now devoted to nautical activities and tourism. It is to be hoped that one day the dam will no longer be an obstruction to navigation along the canal.

On the south side of the lake is the Quénécan Forest, three thousands hectares of beech, spruce and pine. Hidden by the trees are two charming little chapels of Saint-Ignace and Saint-Marc, set in clearings. The trees also hide the heaped ruins of the former Salles Castle, birthplace of the Rohan family, second most important family in Brittany after that of the Breton dukes.

In Mûr-de-Bretagne, the capital of this charming countryside region, is the Saint-Suzanne chapel with its fine collection of statues and enclosure planted with century-old oak trees, which inspired the painter Corot.

Saint-Aignan (Morbihan)

With its porch and its 15th century square tower, the Saint-Aignan church has preserved the rustic charm of its origins. Inside is the Jesse Tree altarpiece, masterpiece of a local workshop, surprisingly delicate yet vigorous and with a touch of humour.

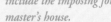

Les Forges des Salles

In the heart of Quénécan Forest, the village of les Forges des Salles stopped its iron and steel making activities in1880. This activity started in the Middle Ages when the local presence of iron ore, wood and water persuaded the Rohan family to build the first furnace. The actual remains, dating mainly from the 18th century, include the imposing forge master's house.

Bon-Repos Abbey

At the confluence of the rivers Daoulas and Blavet, in a setting of quiet beauty, rise the majestic classic walls of the Bon-Repos Abbey. From its foundation in 1184 by a Viscount of Rohan up to the French Revolution, Cistercian monks lived and worked there.

After a long period of abandon, the abbot's lodging is now being patiently restored. To the north, the jagged schist escarpments of the Daoulas Gorges are in sharp contrast with the serenity of the Abbey setting.

Lanrivain

The monumental Guiaudet Fountain has two twin basins surmounted by niches.

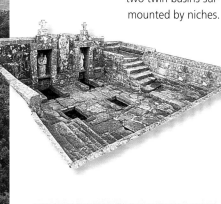

The Daoulas Gorges.

Liscuis passage graves

Above the Daoulas Gorges three passage graves were originally encompassed by a single tumulus. Each one consists of a passage, a burial chamber and a cell. Some five thousand years ago, a local Neolithic community buried its dead here.

Cléguérec (Morbihan)

Near the Trinité chapel at Cléguérec with its fine statues the 16th century fountain is a refined marriage of Flamboyant Gothic and Art Nouveau. Surmounted by a three-cross crucifix the main basin has a pediment decorated with a shell and under the arch is a Trinity group.

Ille-et-Vilaine
A VOYAGE THROUGH BRITTANY

Rennes dominates the Ille-et-Vilaine by its historical, economic, university and demographic importance. In the heart of the city, the resuscitated Parlement de Bretagne building is a symbol of the Breton capital's preeminence, first when it was a Duchy (shared with Nantes), then as a province, and finally as the modern administrative region. But the Ille-et-Vilaine département is not monolithic for all that. Redon looks out towards the Vilaine estuary. Fougères has nostalgic memories of the working-class struggles in the shoe industry. Dinard is so aristocratically British and Saint-Malo is Saint-Malo. The commercial success of the "privateers town", the size and dynamism of its maritime companies, its claims to fame, from Jacques Cartier to Chateaubriand, all seem to have pushed the town to consider itself as a kind of autonomous republic. It is a shame that it has to share some its most beautiful gems. The Rance Valley, the Emerald Coast, the Paimpont Forest which, under its other name of Brocéliande, is alive with Arthurian legends, the Saint-Michel Bay, all these cross département borders with surprising ease. But the Ille-et-Vilaine can console itself as being the only Breton département to have three cathedrals, Rennes, Dol and Saint-Malo, and being able to base its promotional communication on attractions and assets that are as famous as they are varied, from the Cancale oyster to… Madame de Sévigné.

SAINT-LUNAIRE

If Saint-Lunaire was founded by a Welsh monk, the resort was developed at the end of the last century by a banker from Haiti. It is easy to understand how they were both attracted to this beautiful part of the coast, with its succession of beaches and rocky headlands.

From Décollé Point, renown for its eclectically-styled villas in a setting of greenery, there is a superb view of the Emerald Coast.

The legend of Saint-Lunaire

Saint-Lunaire came from Wales. Bishop of a large monastery, he emigrated with his monks in 509. He landed near Décollé Point and immediately started to clear the surrounding land. To fix the limits of his new monastery, the saintly man "threw down his coat on long stones lying on the ground, ordered them to rise and walk and where they stopped were the limits of the monastic grounds".

In the 14th century, a granite slab representing the bishop in full episcopal dress, was added to the Gallo-Roman sarcophage. Saint-Lunaire is invoked to heal eye diseases.

DINARD

Discovered in the last century by rich visitors, sometimes English but also from Paris, the town was soon covered with hotels and impressive villas. The setting had a lot to offer: the mild climate, the combined charms of the Rance estuary and the sea and a multitude of varied view points, the proximity to Saint-Malo. All this encouraged visitors to come to what was originally the simple little village of Saint-Enogat.

Tents, sand, holidays...

The posh headlands, the thalasso, the main beach, villas and flowers.

The Belle Époque has had its day and the resort has become more democratic but the extravagant villas on Moulinet Point and Malouine Point, with their false turrets and unimpeded views, are reminders of a certain art de vivre.

The luxury hotels along the avenue George V still offer their customers a splendid panoramic view of the Rance, the Saint-Malo ramparts and the Solidor Tower.

The Anglican church of Saint-Barthélémy is still visited by the British. The Clair-de-Lune (Moonlight) promenade, with its such evocative name, is a chance to dream offered to all visitors. Dinard will always be Dinard.

The "Belle Époque" villas on Moulinet Point.

SAINT-MALO

A Republic in itself. Jealous of its independence, Saint-Malo has much to justify its pride. The "Messieurs de Saint-Malo", ship owners and privateers, traded with the entire world. Not only was this small island the-birthplace of many a famous and hardy sailor, Jacques Cartier, Duguay-Trouin or Surcouf, but also of some of the most brilliant minds of their time, Chateaubriand or Lamennais.

Chateaubriand
and his tomb
on the Grand Bé.

In the Cour de la Houssaye, the "Duchesse Anne" house, a very fine turreted 15th century dwelling.

The ramparts and the Great Gate.

Gaillard Castle in a storm.

Reminders of the town's glorious past are everywhere. In the Walled City around the cathedral, are fine ship owners town houses. Along the ramparts, the Solidor Tower, watching over the Rance estuary, reminds one of the epic period of sail clippers. Saint-Malo and the sea is a long love affair which is unlikely to die. Proof of this is the enormous success of its Book Festival, *Les étonnants voyageurs*.

Portuguese Navy sail training vessels Creoula and Sagres in the Vauban dock.

Surcouf
1773-1827

CANCALE

Cancale is a double town: on the cliff tops, the main centre and the church and below, la Houle harbour, with its closely packed fishermen's houses, in constant peril from flooding. The town owes its fame to its tasty oysters, full of character like the town's women.

The women had to manage everyday affairs when the men were away at sea fishing around Newfoundland or along the local coast aboard their bisquines.

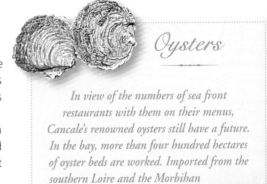

Oysters

In view of the numbers of sea front restaurants with them on their menus, Cancale's renowned oysters still have a future. In the bay, more than four hundred hectares of oyster beds are worked. Imported from the southern Loire and the Morbihan Gulf, the small oysters, flat or hollow, are raised from spat.

At low tide, the real amateurs perpetuate the traditional fishing on foot.

The bisquines are fine sailing boats originally from Normandy. They carry a record surface of sail and have recently been resuscitated by an association who have started organising regattas.

The rocky crest of Grouin Point, 50 metres high, offers a view point of rare beauty. On a clear day, the view extends from Cap Fréhel to the Mont-Saint-Michel !

Houle harbour and the main centre above, dominated by its 1875 Neo-Gothic church.

THE MONT-SAINT-MICHEL
on the Emerald Coast

On the limit between Brittany and Normandy (but on Norman territory!), this has been the home of a Christian community for over one thousand four hundred years. They have given a soul to this exceptional place, renowned as a centre of pilgrimage since the High Middle Ages.

Built in the 10th century on the site of an original sanctuary, the Pre-Romanesque church is the first element of an ingenious and splendid edifice, which has never ceased to expand on this site surrounded by water. The soul of the Mont floats through the Abbey and the numerous monastery buildings, one of which, the cloister, seems suspended between sky and sea. At low tide it is possible to walk around the village and appreciate the ring of defensive structures. At nightfall, empty of its human tide, "The Marvel", becomes its authentic and bewitchingly magic self.

The salt marshes at the foot of the Mont.　　Play of light under the arches of the cloister.　　The Mont in the setting sun.

DOL-DE-BRETAGNE

Dedicated to Saint Samson, the cathedral is a gem of the Gothic-Norman style. Large and elegant, the nave is lit by an impressive stained glass window, one of the oldest in Brittany. In this austere faced edifice, the Italian Renaissance style makes an intrusion in the magnificent 16th century bishop's tomb. The town still has some surviving Mediaeval dwellings, one of which, the Plaids house is a fine example of 12th century civil architecture.

The Champ Dolent standing stone. In the village of Carfentin stands one of Brittany's finest standing stones. It is 9,5 m high and is the source of many a legend.

COMBOURG

Visitors are sometimes unjust to Combourg's former lords and nobility. Of all the gentlemen from past centuries who have built, extended, embellished and sometimes defended the fortress, only one name is remembered: Chateaubriand. In the middle of its extensive grounds, the castle is impressive. The facade and Medieval towers differ greatly from the interior, restored during the last century in a vigorously applied Neo-Gothic style. Clustered around the castle's base, the town still has several interesting old buildings.

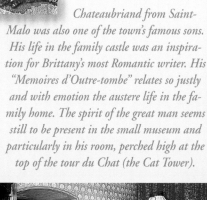

Chateaubriand

Chateaubriand from Saint-Malo was also one of the town's famous sons. His life in the family castle was an inspiration for Brittany's most Romantic writer. His "Memoires d'Outre-tombe" relates so justly and with emotion the austere life in the family home. The spirit of the great man seems still to be present in the small museum and particularly in his room, perched high at the top of the tour du Chat (the Cat Tower).

Cool shade along the Ille-et-Rance Canal near Hédé.

HÉDÉ

At the bottom of Hédé hill, the Ille-et-Rance Canal, opened in 1832, had to negotiate a 25 m drop in level in a distance of two kilometres.

A series of eleven locks were built, about 150 m apart, giving a stunning effect. Ancient trees create a majestic setting for this avenue of water, locks and greenery, unique in Brittany.

BÉCHEREL

Bécherel is in a beautiful setting. A village perched above green countryside, itself dominated by the powerfully elegant spire (1624) of its church. In the past, the local merchants, whose solid 17th and 18th century stone houses can still be admired, made a good living with linen and flax. This "little town of character" is now full of book shops and has become the renowned capital of second-hand books.

The portcullised gateway of Montmuran evokes the waring Middle Ages.

MONTMURAN CASTLE

Montmuran Castle stands proudly overlooking the green countryside. Its origins date from the 12th century, but the portcullised gateway, drawbridge and chapel date from the 14th century. In 1354, according to tradition, Bertrand de Guesclin, after having warded off an attack by followers of Jean de Montfort, during the Breton War of Succession, was knighted on the spot in the chapel. Several years later he married the castle's heir.

FOUGÈRES

I n the bottom of the Nançon Valley, near the frontier of the Kingdom of France, Fougères's fortress defended solidly of one of Brittany's approaches. What an impression of powerful might echoes from its walls!

Built between the 12th and 15th century on a concentric defense plan, the castle has thirteen towers whose names are a colorful mix of legend and history: Mélusine, Raoul, Gobelin, etc. The covered pathway between the towers offers a large panoramic view of the granite houses in the bourg Neuf (new centre) and the Saint-Léonard church situated on the crest of the hill above the river.

Guémadeuc Tower
La Haye Saint-Hilaire Tower
Hallay Tower
Cadran Tower
Guibé Tower
Raoul Tower
Gobelin Tower
Amboise Tower
Mélusine Tower
Surienne Tower

From the 12th century onwards, tanners and later cloth-makers and haberdashers settled in the town along the banks of the river.Sock-makers became manufacturers of woolen slippers and later shoes, establishing the town's industrial renown.

The illuminated castle, and, on the hill, the Saint-Léonard.

Saint-Sulpice

Facing the fortress, the Saint-Sulpice church is a fine example of the Flamboyant Gothic style. Near the south door is the fairy Mélusine brushing her hair. Inside one can admire the fine stone altarpieces and a rather singular decor, conceived in the 13th century, which seems to come straight out of a theatre.

The Guémadeuc, Haye-Saint-Hilaire and Hallay Towers.

VITRÉ

A keep, pepper-box towers and thick curtain walls, steeped in memories of bygone wars, look down over a superb Flamboyant Gothic church (Notre-Dame) and a multitude of half-timbered houses. No town in Brittany is such a powerful reminder of the Middle Ages than Vitré. Built on rocky spur on the Marches of the then Duchy, the castle is a majestic example of Medieval military architecture. Inherited by the Laval family from that of Vitré, the fortress resisted, when, as a Protestant stronghold in 1589, it was besieged by the Ligueurs of the Duke of Mercoeur, Governer of Brittany. The castle now houses the town hall and an interesting museum of local art, archeology and ethnography.

In the former walled town, still partially circled by its ramparts, the buildings in the rue de la Baudrairie and rue d'En Bas have abundant and attractive detailed decorations.

The castle and half-timbered house in the rue d'En Bas.

The Rochers Château

Hidden in the countryside amidst woods and greenery the Rochers Château was an appreciated haven for Madame de Sévigné, when she wanted a break with the extravagant and busy life of the capital. Built during the 14th century and modified during the 17th century, the building has several rooms dedicated to the famous writer. the memory of the Marquis still haunts the French-style gardens and the octogonal chapel built for her uncle and abbot "Le Bien Bon"..

The Rochers Château

RENNES

Rennes the capital. Already in the Middle Ages, the city on the confluent of the Rivers Ille and Vilaine shared with Nantes the honour of having the ducal court and administrative services. Then, after the 1532 Treaty of Union between Brittany and France, it was the home of the governor and intendant who managed the province in the king's name. Finally, now that Nantes is attached to the Pays de Loire administrative region, Rennes is now the uncontested préfecture of the Brittany region, now reduced to four départements.

In the Mediaeval quarter of Rennes, its historical centre, is the Saint-Pierre cathedral, extensively rebuilt in the 18th century, and fine half-timbered houses around the squares of Sainte-Anne and Champ-Jacquet. To the east of this quarter is the classic part of the town, built before and especially after the terrible fire that ravaged the city in 1720.

The place de la Mairie is bordered by two complementary buildings although of different periods. Built by Jacques Gabriel during the reign of Louis XV, the town hall has in its centre a clock tower topped by a elegant Italian-styled campanile. It was almost a century later when the theatre, a fine example of the Neo-Paladian-style, completed the square's layout.

The Breton Parliament building, an emblematic symbol of royal Brittany, and now housing the Law Courts, unfolds the noble symmetry of its facade, designed by Salomon de Brosse during the reign of Louis XIV.

18th century town hall.

Severely damaged in 1994 by fire and water, the Brittany Parliament building has now refound its former splendour. Once again one can marvel at the magnificent paintings and gilding of the coffered ceilings (17th century) in the salle des Pas Perdus and the Grand'Chambre.
Above: The Brittany Parliament building and the place Royale.

The theatre and the Millardet Arcades.

The theatre's ceiling, painted in 1913 by Lemordant, is an example of the diversity of Breton styles.

The greenhouses in the Thabor gardens.

The Thabor Gardens

After visiting the superb collections of the Historical and Fin Arts museums, nothing is better than a stroll through the Thabor Gardens, whose brilliant and sensitive design was the work of the famous Bühler brothers.

The Law Centre

Far from relying on its glorious past, Rennes can also be audacious in its modern architecture, an illustration of which is the new Law Centre. It must be said that its university and high technology complex are sources of constant innovation.

LA ROCHE AUX FÉES

About thirty kilometres south-east of Rennes, in a shaded countryside setting, the Roche-aux-Fées dolmen is an impressive 4500 year old relic of the past. Forty one blocks of stone (the heaviest of which weighs 45 tons?) make up the 19.5 metre-long dolmen, one of Brittany's finest megalithic monuments. It is easy to understand why this "Angevin portico dolmen" has given rise to so many legends. Fairies are said to have transported the rocks here in their veils. They do in fact come from a quarry four kilometres away.

The local rural churches, Retiers, Brie, Visseiche, Piré-sur-Seiche, etc., all have fine marble and tuff 17th century Laval altarpieces, inspired by the Italian mannerism style.

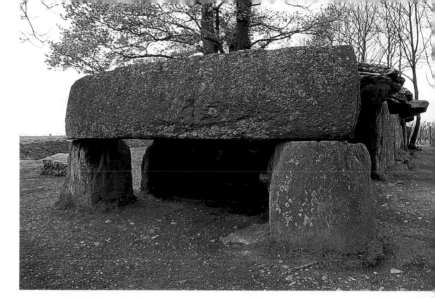

LES PAYS DE LA VILAINE

The steep wooded cluse of the Ile-aux-Pies in the Oust Valley.

Fishing with a square net on the River Vilaine.

The schist and granite landscape along the rivers Vilaine and Oust, its tributary, is a joy to all nature lovers. Near the marshes and the secret hollows of reed beds, cliffs, locally called cluses, such as the superb ones at the Ile-aux-Pies between Saint-Vincent-sur-Oust and Bain-sur-Oust, are exceptional rock climbing sites.

Between river banks covered with pine and chestnut trees, solitary fishermen rediscover ancestral gestures.

REDON

The territorial organisation following the French Revolution was not kind to the Redon pays, straddled between three départements and two regions! Since the foundation, by one of King Nominoë advisers, of its Benedictine abbey in 832, the town has affirmed itself as a centre of Breton spirit and conscience. At the junction of the Nantes to Brest Canal and the River Vilaine, the harbour quarter, with its fine town houses of 17th and 18th century ship owners, now tastefully restored, is an ensemble of urban harmony.

Saint-Sauveur Abbey

Curiously, there are two neighbouring bell towers. The impressive and squat three-level arcaded Romanesque one, unique in Brittany, and the fine Gothic one, separated from the church since a fire in the 18th century. Inside the contrast is equally striking between the dimly-lit Romanesque nave and the bright Gothic chancel. Incorporated into the neighbouring school, the cloisters lack nothing in elegance.

The Redon Pays chestnuts

The memory of the chestnut tree, the true symbol of the Redon pays, is perpetuated in the annual Bogue d'Or (golden chestnut) competition of traditional song. Open to all, both young and old, it is an occasion to bring back to life treasures of popular culture and encourage their future preservation.

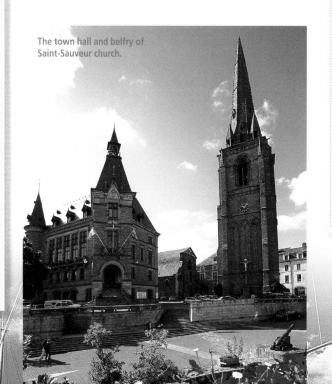

The **town hall and belfry** of Saint-Sauveur church.

The pleasure-craft harbour.

BROCÉLIANDE

The thickets and clearings of the seven thousands hectares of Paimpont Forest, the ancient Brocéliande, still echo with the magic and mystery of the Arthurian legends. Son of a devil and a nun, Merlin is invested with great powers which he uses to the service of Good. Adviser to Uther Pendragon and his son Arthur, he organises the Knights of the Round Table and helps Arthur's companions in their quest for the Holy Grail. Merlin the ma-gician is none the less a man and for his love for Viviane he becomes an eternal prisoner of the beautiful fairy who was once his disciple.

From the Barenton Fountain to the church in Tréhorenteuc, from the Valley of No Return to the Golden Tree, from the Bridge of Secrets to Comper Castle, numerous initiatory circuits take one into the very heart of Breton legend.

Merlin's Tomb

The remains of a megalithic monument, not far from the Fountain of Youth, are said to contain the remains of Merlin the Sorcerer. It is said that long ago the fairy Viviane used a trick to imprison her lover. She said she wanted to be near him after death so he led her to a ditch where he laid down. She immediately dropped the two enormous stones on top of him. Ever since, Merlin the Sorcerer rests in the heart of Brocéliande, imprisoned by a fairy that he had fallen madly in love with.

Trécesson *(Morbihan)*

On the edge of the forest, Trécesson is a strange mix of mystery and poetry. The towers and walls of this late Middle Ages red schist castle stand in a placid pool. Across the moat, a bridge leads to a picturesque gatehouse crowned by a machicolated gallery.

Set majestically on the edge of a vast pool encircled by the forest, Paimpont Abbey has been a place of worship since its foundation by King Judikaël in the 6th century. Inside the Gothic church there are classical wooden furnishings and a superb ivory Christ. Now used by the town council, the presbytery and a social institution, the vast 17th century monastery buildings are a continuation of the charming former village. Far from the bustle of modern life, a visit to Paimpont is a guarantee of back-to-roots peace and quiet.

The Golden Tree

A tree covered with gold leaf, homage to the tree and to those men who defend it.
(permanent structure by François Davin - 1991).

Tréhorenteuc *(Morbihan)*

The white stag surrounded by four lions is the symbol of Christ surrounded by the four Evangelists. It is also the symbol of the Gallic god Kernunnos. Here he is wearing a gold Christian necklace and the lions are both guardians of Paradise and infusers of the Holy Spirit. At some moments we come across pre-Christian mythology. Stag was then food for prehistoric populations, but also a deity that could bring either evil and suffering or wealth and opulence.

The Tréhorenteuc White Stag. (Tréhorenteuc church - White Stag mosaic created in 1955 by Jean Delpech, after a drawing by Odorico).

A stroll in the heart of the forest.

Morbihan
A VOYAGE THROUGH BRITTANY

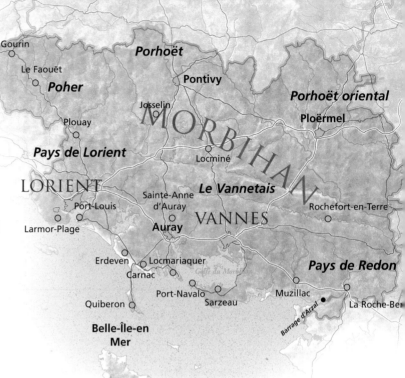

Apparently modest, the Morbihan can boast many first prizes: Carnac, prehistoric capital; Belle-île, queen of the islands; Sainte-Anne d'Auray, mother of all the Breton pardons; La Trinité-sur-Mer, the best sailing waters; the Gulf, the finest inland sea; Quiberon, Mecca of sea water therapy centres. Heading inland, one finds haughty fortresses, chapels of finely carved stone, well cared for rural architecture and rivers and streams that invite you to stroll. Divided between the Breton speaking west and the Gallo speaking east, torn between Lorient the new, the seaward, and Vannes the Episcopal, the secular, for a long time the Morbihan bore the wounds opened up by the Chouannerie (royalist rebellion). It is now reconciled with itself.

PORT-LOUIS

On the estuary of the River Blavet, the turrets of Port-Louis's citadel watch out to sea and over the Lorient roadstead. In 1590 the Spanish troops of Don Juan del Aguila arrived to assist the Duke of Mercoeur, governor of Brittany opposed to Henri IV. They built the citadel in eight years. Richelieu finished the work and Blavet became Port-Louis in honor of Louis XIII. In 1664, consecration for the fortified town: it became the headquarters of the India Company. The fine town houses built for the directors and managers stand with their austere facades along streets as straight as a die.

The citadel - Visiting the ramparts and the fortifications

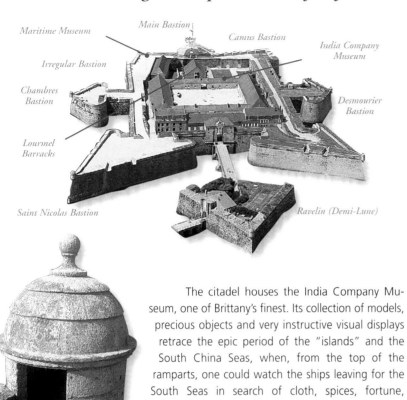

Maritime Museum
Main Bastion
Camus Bastion
India Company Museum
Irregular Bastion
Chambres Bastion
Desmourier Bastion
Lourmel Barracks
Saint Nicolas Bastion
Ravelin (Demi-Lune)

The citadel houses the India Company Museum, one of Brittany's finest. Its collection of models, precious objects and very instructive visual displays retrace the epic period of the "islands" and the South China Seas, when, from the top of the ramparts, one could watch the ships leaving for the South Seas in search of cloth, spices, fortune, adventure and glory.

RIANTEC

Also on the water's edge, the Sainte-Radegonde church in Riantec, although built in 1927 in a Neo-Gothic style, is not without charm with its Arts deco mosaics and its brightly coloured stained glass windows.

THE GÂVRES PENINSULA

Along a quay, a line of fishermen's houses, white and low, some covered with tiles. This extremity of the Gâvres peninsula has something reminiscent of southern France. In the late 19th century Neo-Romantic church, models of three-masted schooners offered as *ex-votos* are reminders of its former seafaring activities. On the headland the view extends over the coast of Larmor-Plage, the island of Groix and, on a clear day, the Wild Coast of the Quiberon Peninsula.

LORIENT

The Cité de la Voile Eric Tabarly is an invitation to discover the invigorating world of ocean racing, its heroes and skippers.

In 1666, a royal ordenance and the determination of Colbert led to the creation of ship building yards between the two streams of Faouëdic and Scorff. In a landscape of heathland, l'Orient (the name of the ship) began its life under the auspices of the India Company. After massive destruction during the last war, Lorient has affirmed itself as a military, commercial, fishing and pleasure-craft port. France's second most important fishing port after Boulogne, its fishing activities are varied, but include industrial trawlers fishing in the North Atlantic.

Onshore activities are concentrated in the Kéroman fishing port whose quays, slipways, warehouses and fish markets are particularly animated during the night.

The "Maison de la Mer" in the marina.

LARMOR-PLAGE

Ideally situated at the entrance of the bay, the villas of Larmor-Plage, Lorient's seaside resort, line the sea front.

Toulhars beach.

Notre-Dame de la Clarté

When a warship crossed the narrow entrance of the Lorient roadstead, it fired a three canon shot salute to Larmor church, which replied with bell rings. Its 1630 fortified tower-belfry and its Apostles Porch are justifiably renowned.

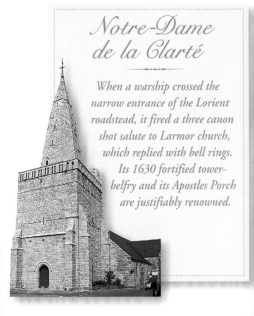

The picturesque little fishing ports along the coast road, Lomener, le Pérello, Kerroc'h, le Courégan, specialise in crustaceans, edible crab and lobster.

Further along, since 1748, the batteries of the small island of Fort Bloqué control a straight part of the coast and the vast Guidel beaches.

Built in 1748, decommissioned in 1855, Fort Bloqué was built to stop the English landing.

Flanked by impressive cliffs, the vast beaches of Guidel are much appreciated by the Lorientais... and others.

Lorient Interceltic Festival

The Celts and music in all its forms: every August, the Lorient Festival brings together thousands of pipers, singers and dancers from Scotland, Cornwall, Wales, Ireland... and Brittany. La fête !

HENNEBONT

Powerful lines of stone, festooned with pinnacles, the basilica Notre-Dame-du-Paradis was built in the early 16th century on the initiative of a blacksmith. Around the Medieval Bro-Erec'h porch, flanked by twin towers, floats the memory of the wife of Jean de Montfort, Jehane de Flandres. Intrepid defender of the town during the Breton War of Succession, she became known as Jehanne la Flamme.

Since 1857 the Hennebont stud farm, which takes part in the selection of future Breton breed stallions, is established in the former Notre-Dame-de-la-Joie Abbey.

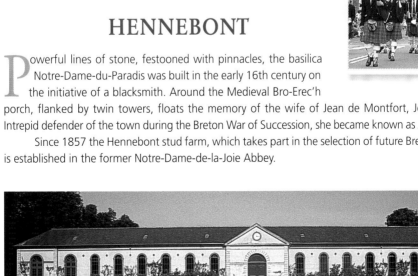

GROIX ISLAND

It is difficult to forget of the glorious past of the Island of Groix. At the beginning of the century it was France's most important tunny fishing port with a fleet of some two hundred Dundees with their majestic rigs. A museum recalls this epic period and does not forget the women who worked both on the land and in the canning factories. If the tunny campaigns have had there day and the men of Groix moved to the port of Keroman in Lorient, the island holds on jealously to its identity. At the foot of its cliffs, like in the Trou de l'Enfer (Hell's Hole), the water rumbles in nervous eddies.

J.-P. Calloc'h

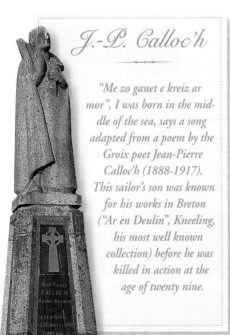

"Me zo ganet e kreiz ar mor", I was born in the middle of the sea, says a song adapted from a poem by the Groix poet Jean-Pierre Calloc'h (1888-1917). This sailor's son was known for his works in Breton ("Ar en Deulin", Kneeling, his most well known collection) before he was killed in action at the age of twenty nine.

A nature reserve now protects the surprisingly rich mineral resources. At Port-Tudy the main activity is now inshore fishing with small fishing smacks and trawlers. Along the island's narrow roads one can discover numerous construction relating to the sea: lighthouses, former canning factories, quays, fish pens, lifeboat stations…, all reminders of the close communion between man and the sea.

An old-fashioned sailing boat entering Port-Tudy harbour, marked by its symetric lights on the quays.

THE ISLANDS OF HOUAT, AND HŒDIC

The "ocean sisters"

Aerial view of the Island of Houat.

Aerial view of the Island of Hoedic.

Hoedic Fort, built in 1847 by order of Louis-Philippe, as defence against the English.
Below: Port Collet, built in 1818, as a shelter for Houat Island's boats.

H ouat and Hoedic, big and small in old Celt, duck and duckling according to a more fanciful but well anchored etymological interpretation, precious flowers in Brittany's seaward meadows.

In the continuation of the Quiberon Peninsula and the Béniguet reef are two comma-liked bare pieces of land, with low dry stone houses huddled together and arcs of cliffs and beaches. Hardly more than five hundred inhabitants between them.

Houat, home of the stern and everlasting yellow carnation, counts on shrimp fishing and crustacean farms for its future development. After having been invaded several times over the centuries, mainly by the English - the number of forts scattered along the coasts of both islands are an eloquent reminder - Houat and Hoëdic are determined not to lose their souls because of tourism. The Conservatoire du littoral (coastal conservation agency), keeps watch over the coast and marshes, the sea lily, the wild carnations and tamarisk. It is important to preserve a way of life and moral values as an example to future generations.

BELLE-ÎLE-EN-MER

Certainly the most beautiful. So precious was the island that it was an asset hotely disputed between several Breton abbeys; and that the famous Superintendent Fouquet, when he became Marquis of Belle-île, and shortly before he was disgraced, had established ambitious projects for his island domain. The English occupied the island several times, but less often than the number of times they besieged it. Driven out of America in the mid 18th century, Arcadians found refuge on the island and some still have descendants there. At the height of her glory, Sarah Bernhardt fell in love with the place and converted a fort into her island home.

Le Palais. The quays of the inner harbour dominated by the Christ-Roi church.

The entrance to Palais harbour.

The western wild coast and the Port-Coton Needles.

Poulains Point.

The Vauban Citadel

Cavalary path

Rampart Barracks

Bastion

Ravelin (Demi-Lune)

Counterban

Arsenal

Side Bastion

Bank

Curtain

Ditch

Powderhouse

One would like to sing praise to everything: the rampart of rugged cut cliffs, the small valleys of flamboyant yellow broom edging down to solitary creeks, the Apothecary Grotto where the sea comes crashing in, the long whitewashed houses, the oriental charm of Locmaria church, Palais harbour and its ria watched over by guardian angels, the thousand and one marvels of Brittany's largest island.

If the Palais citadel evokes Vauban's military art, the small harbour of Sauzon and its yellow, pink and ochre roughcast cottages seem to transport one to a Greek island.

Locmaria church.

Donnant

Goulphar

Pointe du Grand Guet

Bangor

Pointe du Skeul

Locmaria

Pointe d'Arzic

Port An Dro

Belle-Ile is the largest Breton island. 17 km long and between 5 and 9 km wide,
it lies parallel to the mainland, 30 km out to sea. During the summer,
its two ports, Le Palais and Sauzon, welcome the boats bringing day visitors
coming to discover the "well-named island".

Pointe de Kerdonis

Pointe des Poulains

Sauzon

Le Palais

Belle Fontaine

Port Yorc'k

Les Grands Sables

Below: The harbours of Sauzon and Le Palais.

QUIBERON

On a narrow piece of land, a miniature Brittany, a peninsula with two identities. Quiberon is above all the carefree, colourful and sometimes smart sailing fraternity atmosphere of an immense seaside resort, with its succession of beaches lined by apartment buildings or villas, pleasure-craft harbours always full, its night life and festivities. It is also the renowned National Sailing Centre and a sea water therapy centre founded by the champion cyclist Louison Bobet. On one most appreciated stretches of sailing water on the Atlantic coast, regattas and competitions of all sorts follow one after the other from April to November.

And then, hardly a stone's throw away, facing west, from Beg an Aud to Beg er Lan, is the Côte Sauvage, the wild coast. A coast of jagged cliffs, of elements in furry, waves crashing in like thunder. A vision sometimes Dantesque, always invigorating, of the eternal battle between the ocean and land.

Ceramic bas-relief decorating the front of the "Viviers Quiberonnais".

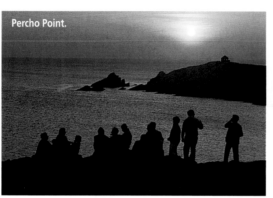

Percho Point.

The Port-Blanc Arch.

Port-Maria.

Port-Haliguen lighthouse.

The PENTHIÈVRE *fortress*

Placed like a sentry at the entrance to the peninsula, Penthièvre Fort was built in 1747 after a devastating invasion by the English. It made history in 1795. Besieged by General Hoche and his Republican troops, the Royalists having landed and occupied the fort then capitulated. Despite promises of clemency, more than seven hundred noblemen were executed.

Port-Maria lighthouse.

Sheltered by pine trees, Saint-Pierre-de-Quiberon beach.

With its two harbours, Port-Haliguen and Port-Maria, and a dozen canning factories, Quiberon was France's most important sardine fishing port after the war. Now fishing is only with small boats with one or two men on board, bringing in fine fish such as bass, gilt-head, conger and crustaceans - and scallops during the winter.

Turpault Castle

This strange edifice was built in 1904 by a mill owner from Cholet, Georges Turpault. He has left his name as the sounding buoy of Quiberon. On very windy days one says, "It's Turpault cow mooing".

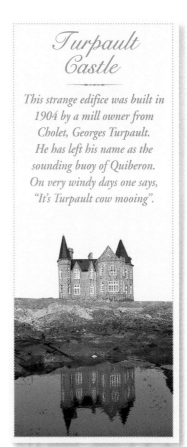

The main beach of Port-Maria.

LA TRINITÉ-SUR-MER

With over a thousands places, La Trinité-sur-Mer with Le Crouesty is Morbihan's biggest marina, and almost certainly the best loved by all sailors. Since Eric Tabarly (1931-1998) won his first single-handed Transatlantic race in 1964, bringing renown to the port, La Trinité has become a favourite rendezvous for skippers.

The former fishing harbour in the evening light.

Kerispert Bridge and marina on the River Crac'h.

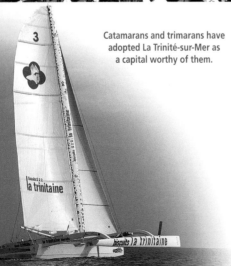

Catamarans and trimarans have adopted La Trinité-sur-Mer as a capital worthy of them.

Elves on board ship

They are very small, black and very agile. They do deceitful things on board. It is they that undo the sheets, drop the sails suddenly, jump on sailors and pull their ears so that they swallow their chewing tobacco. Sometimes though, when the boat is clean, they know how to read the compass and wake up the man at the helm who has fallen asleep.

Kervillen beach.

All this activity makes one forget that not long ago La Trinité had a triple activity, now disappeared (apart from a few coastal fishing boats), fishing, merchant trading, and salt production. From the top of Kerispert Bridge, rebuilt in 1958, there is a superb view over the forest of masts and the oyster beds along the River Crac'h. From May to September, numerous sailing races, trophies, regattas and old riggers festivals animate the river.

Immortalised by Eric Tabarly, Pen Duick was designed in 1898 by the naval architect William Fife.

The hollow oyster

Oyster beds flourish in the sheltered waters of the estuaries of La Trinité-sur-Mer, Saint-Philibert and Locmariaquer. Attacked by two successive illnesses, the flat oyster was replaced by the Portugese hollow oyster until 1970, and then by Japonese ones. Once collected, the spat are sent to Saint-Brieuc Bay.

On the river bank, the parish church and the fountain.

SAINT-PHILIBERT

Spread along the banks of a small estuary, the village of Saint-Philibert, formerly a part of Locmariaquer, has built its reputation on the oyster.

Standing near the Fontaine aux Bêtes (beasts fountain), the simple architecture of its church, in an agreeable setting above the river, hides an impressive classical altarpiece. Along the coastal footpaths, one can discover the Kerlioret tidal mill, the Kernevest lighthouse (1856) and fort (1885), the Kercadoret pool, now a nature reserve.

CARNAC

The name of Carnac will forever foster dreams. Its four thousand standing stones, its dolmens, mounds and tumuli have unveiled only a small part of their mystery. These standing stones, erected during Neolithic times, between 5000 and 2000 years BC., have given rise to many a theory, ranging from the strictly reasonable to the completely cranky.

The dolmens, we know, were burial places for nobles and chiefs, but erosion over the centuries has changed their original appearance. The large flat covering slabs are remains of what was a closed structure, completed by additional dry-stone work and reinforced by a mound of earth or small rocks.

The Menec Lines.

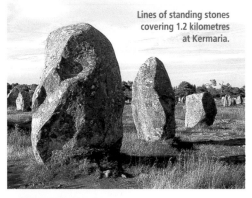
Lines of standing stones covering 1.2 kilometres at Kermaria.

Imposing megalithic chamber at Crucuno.

The Saint-Michel chapel and tumulus.

On the other hand, the exact finality of the lines of Ménec, Kerlescan and Kermario will undoubtedly remain unknown for years to come. Astronomic observatories, primitive places of worship? Perhaps. But until all this becomes clear, it has become important to safeguard these megalithic sites, so often threatened by excessive tourist access. Ambitious conservation measures are being undertaken to restore the alignments and archaeological digs are being continued, bringing new light to bear on our knowledge of the funeral rites of these fascinating Neolithic populations.

Saint Cornély

Saint Cornély is the Breton name of Saint Corneille, Roman Pope in the year 251. Cornély, by a play of words with corns, has become the patron saint of cows and bulls. Up until the last war, the animals decorated with ribbons, were taken to the fountain and copiously splashed with water. A tuft of hair from the animal's tail was offered to the saint to insure their protection for the year ahead.

Ideally situated on the inner part of Quiberon Bay, Carnac-Plage has become one of the Morbihan's most important seaside resorts. If the main beach seems too crowded for you, you might chose the more family atmosphere of Saint-Colomban beach.

The beach's sailing centre.

Saint-Colomban beach.

AURAY

At the bottom of Auray Hill, the harbour of Saint-Goustan is a marriage of historical memories and a picturesque setting. An old bridge, crossing the Loc'h River at the point where the tide loses its force, leads to a small square of bumpy cobblestones, surrounded by steep roofs and corbelled façades. Steep narrow streets, lined with carefully restored half-timbered houses, climb the hill towards Saint-Sauveur church. In bygone times the harbour was full of sloops and coastal luggers. On the 4th of December 1776, a famous visitor landed from the Reprisal: Benjamin Franklin had come to ask Louis XVI for military aid to kick the English out of America.

Saint-Goustan harbour and its old 15th century bridge.

Saint-Avoye Chapel (1554 -1650)

This chapel in Pluneret, built in one go in the middle of the 16th century, houses a particularly elegant Renaissance rood-loft. The calvary group crowns the gallery where, on the nave side, are statues of the Twelve Apostles in alcoves, separated by pilasters.

LOCMARIAQUER

In Locmariaquer the megalithic is monumental. Here Neolithic giants rub shoulders, sometimes struck down like the Grand Menhir, twenty metres high, three hundred tons, before its fall. The Table des Marchands (Merchants Table) dolmen is decorated in its base by a pointed slab in the form an idol where four rows of shepherds crooks form elegant arabesques.

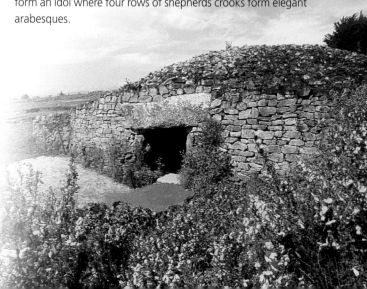

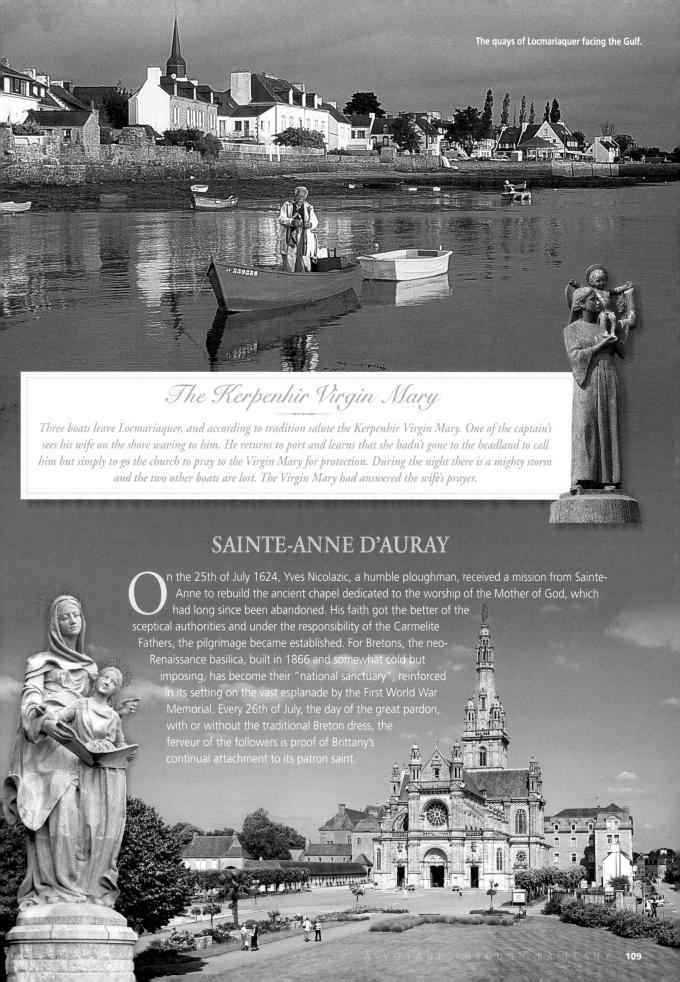

The Kerpenhir Virgin Mary

Three boats leave Locmariaquer, and according to tradition salute the Kerpenhir Virgin Mary. One of the captain's sees his wife on the shore waving to him. He returns to port and learns that she hadn't gone to the headland to call him but simply to go the church to pray to the Virgin Mary for protection. During the night there is a mighty storm and the two other boats are lost. The Virgin Mary had answered the wife's prayer.

SAINTE-ANNE D'AURAY

On the 25th of July 1624, Yves Nicolazic, a humble ploughman, received a mission from Sainte-Anne to rebuild the ancient chapel dedicated to the worship of the Mother of God, which had long since been abandoned. His faith got the better of the sceptical authorities and under the responsibility of the Carmelite Fathers, the pilgrimage became established. For Bretons, the neo-Renaissance basilica, built in 1866 and somewhat cold but imposing, has become their "national sanctuary", reinforced in its setting on the vast esplanade by the First World War Memorial. Every 26th of July, the day of the great pardon, with or without the traditional Breton dress, the ferveur of the followers is proof of Brittany's continual attachment to its patron saint.

ÉTEL

On Étel's quays, in the midst of lobster pots and pungent smells, there is still the atmosphere reminiscent of the great tunny fishing tradition (there were up to 140 boats), now replaced by a more diversified activity. Its famous bar, a constantly changing sand bank, has claimed many victims. In everybody's memory is the drama in 1958 when the lifeboat overturned when going to the aid of Dr. Bombard.

Upstream the silted river is an inland estuary peppered with small islands and criss-crossed by capricious channels. Further inland the river crosses subtly charming countryside, where crops are festooned with seaweed and where sparrows and waders share the same feeding grounds. What a contrast with the vast beaches of Erdeven and its sand dunes, some of southern Brittany's best preserved!

Kerhillio beach at Erdeven.

Pont-Lorois

The Pont-Lorois Bridge, crossing the River Étel between Belz and Plouhinec, has known many trials and tribulations. Built in 1841 by the préfet Lorois - and inaugurated without a benediction, to the great displeasure of the Catholics - the first bridge broke up during a violent storm in 1894. The following bridge was destroyed by the Allies in 1944. The present metal-roadway bridge was built in 1956. From its middle, the view spreads out over the river, its channels and the oyster beds.

SAINT-CADO

On a small island on the River Étel, at the foot of a former sanctuary, the oyster-farming village of Saint-Cado is one of the Morbihan coast's most charming settings. The village was named after a Welsh monk, chased from his home by a Saxon invasion. He set up a hermitage here in 525. Reclaimed from the mud flats, a curved road leads to the island. On a grass-covered hill, the humble Romanesque chapel, extended in the 16th century, houses "Saint Cado's bed", a curious stone monument reputed to be able to cure deafness.

The Legend of Saint Cado

Saint Cado lived on an island on the River Étel as a hermit. When it became necessary to built a dike, the Devil offered to build it in one night in exchange for the soul of the first living being that crossed it. The next morning the Devil's only payment was a black cat that Saint Cado had thrown onto the road ! That is how "monsieur de Kersatan" was fooled.

PLOUHINEC : *Le Vieux Passage*

Between étel and Pont-Lorois, the charming little harbour of Vieux Passage - attached to the commune of Plouhinec - is nestled in a creek on the right-hand bank of the River Étel. It is the kind of peaceful haven, lined by old fishermen's cottages converted into agreeable homes, appreciated as a retirement home or by pleasure-craft owners.

BAUD

On the day of the pardon of Notre-Dame-de-la-Clarté, followers wash their eyes with the water from the charming 16th century fountain, to preserve or cure their eyesight. The origins of the 2.2 metre-high statue of Quinipily are much less catholic. Roman deity, Egyptian, Celtic?

Since the 18th century it thrones on the top of a monumental fountain.

PONT-SCORFF

Important lords of Pont-Scorff during the Ancien Regime, the princes of Rohan-Guéméné built a magnificent Renaissance manor with carved ornamental windows. A little upstream, the Leslé Mill is in a delightful setting on the River Scorff. It was used to crush oak wood and chestnut to make tan used in the leather trade.

Pont-Scorff Zoo

In a vast park near Kerrousseau Mill, one can visit one of Europe's finest collection of big cats, a snake house and a farm of miniature animals.

In the 18th century an Alsacian built the Leslé tan mill on the River Scorff.

KERNASCLÉDEN

The magnificence of Notre-Dame-de-Kernascléden, a masterpiece of Flamboyant Gothic architecture, is witness to the generous patronage of the Dukes of Brittany and the 15th century Rohan family. Inside, the frescos of the Macabre Dance give details of the agonies of Hell.

But the grace of angelic musicians reminds us that even during the Middle Ages Christian teaching was not reduced to the simple fear of the hereafter.

GOURIN

The classic 18th and 19th century Tronjoly Castle is now used for exhibitions.

PLOUAY

Ménéhouarn Castle and its domestic chapel, dedicated to Notre-Dame de Sion, were built in the 18th century by the Pluvié family.

The 16th century covered market.

LE FAOUËT

The subtle but solid architecture of beams and joists of Le Faouët's 16th century covered market is Brittany's finest. This enormous inverted ship's hull form, crowned by and octagonal belfry, is witness to the important fairs and markets that were held there. The former Ursuline Convent now houses a art museum dedicated to artists, who, for a century, have found inspiration in the region.

A gem of Gothic architecture (1489-1512) crammed on a narrow platform overlooking an overgrown ravine, the Sainte-Barbe chapel has the most original setting of any of Brittany's religious monuments. Majestic balustraded stairs built around 1700 give the sanctuary a somewhat surprisingly theatrical look. The stained glass windows and the organ loft, with its delicate angelic musicians are both unexpected and refined for this quiet part of Cornouaille.

Representation of one of Sainte Barbe's miracles.

The Sainte-Barbe chapel.

The Saint-Fiacre rood screen

An absolute masterpiece of the 15th century. The talent of the sculptor, Olivier Le Loergan, was such that he was knighted by Duke François II. On the gallery there is both the sacred and the grotesque. Chickens and pixies, lovers on the binge and drunkards are side by side with the Virgin Mary and the saints, in a wooden fretwork which is a feast for the eyes. These illustrations talk of a popular religion where references to dogma and the truculence of the congregation happily coexist.

Saint-Fiacre chapel
(15th-16th century).

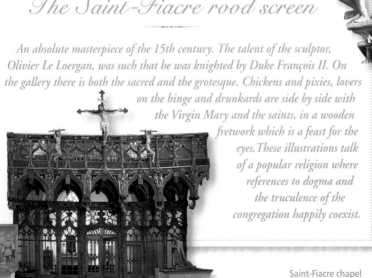

VANNES

Vannes is proud of its past. Few Breton towns have managed to preserve and highlight so many elements of its thousand year history. Originally capital of a Gallic tribe, then a Gallo-Roman town, seat of a bishopric, capital of Nominoë, the first Breton king, town of the union between Brittany and France in 1532, refuge for the exiled Breton Parliament in 1675, and finally préfecture, Vannes has collected as many titles as it has historic remains. Two museums remind us of this glorious past, the Archaeological Museum, and in the Medieval market halls, the Cohue Museum.

The pleasure-craft harbour.

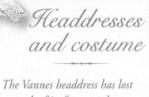

Headdresses and costume

The Vannes headdress has lost much of its former volume. Folded above the forehead, it seems to be delicately placed ready to blow away at any moment.

Old half-timbered houses.

The Medieval festival

In mid July every year, Vannes displays its glorious Medieval past in a festival of costumed processions and knightly jousting tournaments.

The gardens in front of the Hermine Castle.

Saint-Vincent's Gate, built in 1704, crowned with a statue of Saint Vincent Ferrier.

Below, near the harbour, the Saint Vincent's Gate is classically elegant. The eastern line of ramparts, whose curtain walls form a powerful protective shield for the Constable's Tower, have at their foot superb French-style gardens.

Concentrated in a small area, there are half-timbered houses (delightful place Henri IV), sober town houses of former clergymen and parliamentarians, and the 16th century Prison Gate.

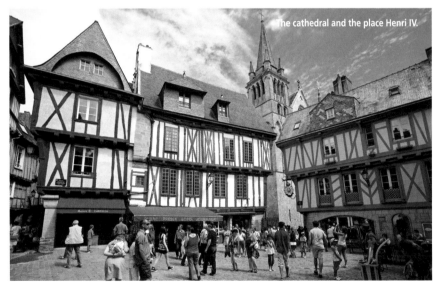

The cathedral and the place Henri IV.

Saint-Pierre Cathedral

The Gothic Saint-Pierre cathedral had the chapel of the Saint-Sacrement, a gem of the Renaissance style, added to it in 1537. Inside are the relics of Saint Vincent Ferrier, a Spanish preacher who died in Vannes in 1419.

MORBIHAN GULF

A tamed ocean. A marine lake peppered with small islands, a sweetly tonic miniature sea, but falsely calm. Go and meditate in the maze of its small creeks but beware of its particularly strong currents.

Arradon, the little harbour of Pen-er-Men at low tide.

Conleau harbour.

Séné-Port-Anna, leaving for the island of Arz.

If fishing still survives in the western parts of the Gulf, the eastern mud banks are a refuge for numerous seabirds. Everywhere, megalithic monuments mark this country, invaded by the sea after their erection. Kingdom of the unexpected and the untiring renewal of nature's spectacle.

Gavrinis

The small island of Gavrinis is the setting for a masterpiece of megalithic art, a cairn or dolmen dating from 4 000 years BC. The upright supporting blocks are decorated with carved geometrical motifs. Are the concentric spirals and circles representations of fertility or of some primitive idol ?

The Er Lannic cromlec'h

The first occupation of the site goes back about 5000 years. Hundreds of pieces of pottery, flints, polished axes, grindstones and cutting wheels have been found there. The cromlec'h is a structure of two tangent circles of standing stones one of which is partly submerged below the Gulf's waters, and the other completely submerged. This phenomena is due to the slow rise in sea level since the last Ice Age.

Where tourism and property development has not yet taken possession of the coastal fringe, fields go right down to the strand, mud banks become marshes. Brannec, Illuric, Stibiden, Creizic, Ilur... the small islands sometimes have names that have a raw Celtic ring about them.

Pomper Mill on the Vannes to Larmor-Baden road.

The islands of Govihan, then Brannec, then Moines Island (its southern part), then, on the right, Creizic: names sounding like a marine nursery rhyme.

Larmor-Baden, a calm sea on a mild evening.

MOINES ISLAND

Six kilometres long, the Gulf's largest island radiates happiness. In this small half-countryside, half-sea paradise, everything seems to welcome the visitor with mild kindness: the main centre and its harmonious captains' houses, the Mediterranean flora of mimosa and fig trees, the narrow footpaths leading to solitary forgotten creeks, the villas covered with vegetation, and even the peaceful marine graveyard. And everywhere, never the same, views over the Gulf. If coastal luggers have long since disappeared along with the elegant headdresses of the island's women, renowned for their beauty, the soft luminous grace of the island will never cease to charm.

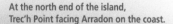

At the north end of the island, Trec'h Point facing Arradon on the coast.

At the foot of the early 20th century villas, pleasure-craft find a natural anchorage in the creek at Lério.

ISLAND OF ARZ

The attraction of the island of Arz is more subtle than its neighbour. Tough and feared, its ocean-going and coastal seamen gave the island the nickname of the island of captains. They shared power on the island with the monks of the priory which was dependent on the Abbey of Saint-Gildas de Rhuys. The solid classical building of the prior's lodgings now houses the town hall and school. The church of the Nativité de Notre-Dame, in part of Romanesque style, has curious capitals of fantastic bestiary. The women use to pray to the 20th century statue of Notre-Dame d'Espérance, for the safe return of their men from sea. In the main centre as well as in the villages, such as Pennéro, simple sailors houses and more imposing ship owners houses are neighbours.

Arriving from the island of Conleau, boats dock at Béluré Point.

Brouel beach is situated in one of the island's wildest parts.

RHUYS PENINSULA

The Morbihan's most important marina with a capacity of one thousand two hundred places, Le Crouesty was built from 1973 onwards in a marshy creek on the south coast of Arzano. Accommodation structures developed along with the port facilities, as well as a sea water therapy centre with its "ocean liner" like architecture.

Le Crouesty marina.

At Sarzeau, the hamlet of Kérolet is ideally situated on the shores of the Gulf.

Saint-Armel, le Passage.

At Saint-Armel, on the western edge of the Gulf, the small island of le Passage is linked to the mainland. It is surrounded by oyster beds, former salt pans and vast mud flats much appreciated by the numerous seabirds.

At the entrance to the Gulf, Port-Navalo still has a few fishing boats and a small museum, housed in the fish auction market. From the foot of its lighthouse (1891), the view spreads out over the Gulf and its strong currents.

Port-Navalo, Port-Noalan beach.

Saint-Gildas-de-Rhuys

Brittany is relatively poor in Romanesque art. Despite the 18th century reconstruction of the belfry, nave and vestibule, in a boring style typical of the period, the Saint-Gildas-de-Rhuys abbey church is an essential reference of religious art. It is in the chevet than one can best appreciate the sober 11th century architecture. The capitaled pillars that separate the chancel from the ambulatory give grace to the antique edifice.

The oyster beds have colonised the creeks and nooks along the River Penerf. After the 1974 epidemic the Portuguese oysters were replaced by a more resistant variety, Japanese gigas. On the opposite bank, at Penvins Point, the chapel of Notre-Dame-de-la-Côte commands an exceptional view over the coast.

Penvins chapel.

A stone's throw from the ocean, one of the favourite residences of the Dukes of Brittany, from Pierre de Dreux to Jean V, was not only a formidable fortress but also an agreeable home. For two and a half centuries, from the 13th to the 15th century, Suscinio became more and more fortified and embellished. In the shadows of its towers, watching over the coastline, and because of the proximity of marshes and forest, the Dukes were enthusiastic hunters.

Despite damage caused in 1798, the castle still has a proud appearance. The interior, housing a fine history museum, has been extensively restored. The stone paving (about 1330) in the ancient chapel still has its bright animal decorations.

Suscinio Castle.

Equestrian statue of Olivier de Clisson.

JOSSELIN

Without doubt the emblematic edifice of the Argoat, Josselin Castle is a flamboyant summary of Medieval Brittany. Seen from the canalised River Oust that flows at its base, it is a haughty fortress solidly anchored on its rock, built at the end of the 14th century by Olivier de Clisson. In absolute contrast, the inside facade, built between 1490 and 1505 by Jean II de Rohan, explodes with Flamboyant Gothic ornamentation of lis, ermines and fabulous animals carved around its massive dormer windows and balustrades. But Josselin is not only the Rohan's castle. The basilica of Notre-Dame-du Roncier with its 17th century organ and cenotaph of Constable Olivier de Clisson and his wife, and the numerous half-timbered houses in the old streets, are also worth of attention.

The late 15th century fireplace in the main salon, illustrated with the Rohan family motto: "A plus" (To More) carved on the mantelpiece.

Each of the massive two storey dormer windows are elaborately decorated with lis, the Rohan mascles, arabesques...

PONTIVY

On it's grassy hill overlooking the River Blavet, the two massive towers and curtain walls of Pontivy Castle stand above the dried-up moat. Built at the end of the 15th century by Jean II of Rohan, later modernised, the fortress became the capital of and stronghold of this powerful family and has never changed hands.

The town has a double somewhat surprising aspect. Firstly the layout of the Medieval streets with their central gutter, lined with half-timbered houses and Renaissance town houses. Next to this is the modern town with its more imperial layout, decided by Napoleon to counteract the Royalist influence in Brittany. The town hall, the law courts and the army barracks, severely grand, are reminders of the time when Pontivy was called… Napoléonville.

Sainte Noyale

Daughter of a king in Great Britain, Sainte Noyale crossed the channel on the branch of a tree. The seigneur Nizan, that she refused to marry, had her beheaded. Miracle, she took her head in her hands and went to the site of the future Saint-Noyale chapel, that she chose as her burial place.

The Rohan's castle (11th and 17th century).

Saint-Sauveur Church in Locminé

Saint-Sauveur church in Locminé is surprising: a large contemporary structure of reinforced concrete and visible wooden beams, inaugurated in 1975, is built against the Gothic portals of the previous building. Among the rare remains that have been preserved is the Vraie Croix altarpiece.

PLOËRMEL

Established on the River Yvel, the Duke's pond extends into the green countryside around Ploërmel. Property of the Dukes of Brittany from 1257 to the end of the Duchy, as were the great mills, the "lake" is now a water sports centre.

ROCHEFORT EN-TERRE

Built up the sides of a rocky schist promontory, the little town of Rochefort-en-Terre has carefully preserved much of its ancient self. Through the flower-decked streets one can see 16th to 18th century town houses, the Seneschal's house, the horse-shoe-shaped covered market, the Romanesque and Gothic Notre-Dame-de-la-Tronchaye church, the calvary huddled around a Crucifixion, the well, turrets, half-timbered houses, all parts of a recomposed past. Alfred Klots, an American painter was at the origin of Rochefort's rebirth. He discovered the town in 1903, built the castle on the site of a former fortress destroyed during the French Revolution and persuaded the people of Rochefort of the importance of preserving their heritage. Open to the public, his house contains a collection of paintings, furniture and other rare objects.

MALESTROIT

Since 1830 the River Oust and the Nantes to Brest Canal become one around Malestroit. Along its-course, through green countryside, pleasure-craft drift quietly past beside the tow path.

Questembert covered market

Built in 1675, the oak-framed covered market forms an impressive three-naved structure fifty five metres long and fifteen metres wide. It is particularly precious and important because many of Brittany's former covered markets have disappeared.

LA GACILLY

The River Aff flows through La Gacilly, a small flowerdecked town of craftsmen and renown today for its Yves Rocher cosmetics laboratory (whose botanical gardens are open to the public).

LA ROCHE-BERNARD

From the top of the old bridge across the River Vilaine, it is difficult to imagine that in La Roche Bernard there is a ancient quarter of patrician houses, like the 16th century Canon's House and other fine dwellings with ornate dormer windows or moulded doorways. A narrow picturesque street goes down the hill to the River Vilaine where the harbour is nestled in a small creek.

MUZILLAC

On the overgrown banks of a pond is the Pen Mur rag paper mill, formerly a flour mill, but now perpetuating an old Breton tradition.

Arzal

Inaugurated in 1972, the 390 meter long Arzal Dam, loved or hated, was built to tame the waters of the River Vilaine.
As a result, a large harbour area has created a boom in pleasure-craft activities on both banks. But, to the detriment of the mussel farmers and fisherman of Tréhiguier, the dam is accelerating the silting up of the Vilaine estuary.

The red-coloured cliffs of Bile Point in Pénestin facing oyster and mussel beds.

Loire-Atlantique
A VOYAGE THROUGH BRITTANY

The Nantes metropolis and its industrial and port ramifications of Donges-Saint-Nazaire have left their mark on the Loire Atlantique, being astride two cultures, Breton to the north and Vendée to the south. The Brière and the Guérande peninsula have established a certain vigorous autonomy, reinforced by their past attachment to the Breton speaking zone. Duchess Anne was born in Nantes, but the vineyards belong to the old League country, the pays de Retz is turned towards the Poitou, Clisson has attachments to Italy and Châteaubriant to the court of François I. Needless to say that the Loire-Atlantique has always been a crossroads, a land of marches.

Map labels: Châteaubria... / LOIRE ATLANTIQUE / Pays de la M... / Pays de Redon / Pays de Loire-Maritime / La Brière / Piriac-sur-Mer / Guérande / La Turballe / Le Croisic / Batz-sur-Mer / Le Pouliguen / La Baule / Pornichet / SAINT-NAZAIRE / La Loire / Pays nanta... / NANTES

La Turballe, returning to port.

LA CÔTE D'AMOUR

Since 1913 the coast of the Guérande peninsula between Saint-Molf and Saint-Nazaire has been known under the charming name of the Côte d'Amour (the coast of love). The development of the La Baule and its surroundings as a holiday resort only dates from the middle of the 19th century, but Le Croisic and La Turballe already had a flattering reputation as trading and fishing ports since the Middle Ages. Along this coastline of many contrasts, rocky headlands and sandy dunes succeed, old church belfries watch over salt marshes, museums of local traditions and pleasure-craft harbours are side by side.

The classical church of Piriac-sur-Mer watches over a fleet of fishing boats, much diminished since the great cod fishing era. Several 17th and 18th century ship owners' houses are reminders of that heroic period. The pleasure-craft owners and holiday makers who have now taken over were preceded by several famous writers, Gustave Flaubert, Alphonse and Léon Daudet, Emile Zola.

Traditional sloop "Le Grand Norven".

Castelli Point.

The port of Piriac-sur-Mer and the 18th century church in the setting sun.

From Castelli Point, once inhabited, according to legend, by elves, there is and splendid view over the wild coast and its strangely named rocks: *Almanzor's Tomb, the Pillows, the mad monk's Hole, the Pipe, Madam's Grotto…*

Fish auction market, cooperative, ultra modern fleet: since 1970, La Turballe has developed all it can to compete with Le Croisic as the Loire-Atlantique's most important fishing port.

La Turballe - unloading the catch of sardines in the Loire-Atlantique's most important fishing port.

Housed on the roof of the fish market, the "maison de la pêche" combines the joys of discovering this fascinating world and gastronomy (sea food restaurant). Although La Turballe's last canning factory closed in 1989, the atmosphere along the quays still has that tangy taste of salt and the open sea. To the south, a five-kilometre-long beach has managed to resist the fever of modern anarchical urban development.

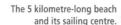

The 5 kilometre-long beach and its sailing centre.

129

GUÉRANDE

The Guérande ramparts, circling the town completely, offer a formidable vision of the Middle Ages. Four gates, eleven towers and impressive curtain walls, the Breton Duchy of the 14th and 15th centuries vigorously affirms and defends itself in the heart of this prosperous peninsula. Grain, vines, salt, fish, and trading, all are successful on this ideally situated coast not far from Nantes, between the Loire and Vilaine estuaries.

The local governor was lodged in Saint Michel's Gate, a magnificent lesson of military architecture with its machicolations, arrow slits and crenellations. It houses the Guérande museum and its collection of sumptuous Saillé and Batz salt workers costumes. An outside boulevard allows one to admire the other gates, Vannetais, Bizienne and de Saillé, as well as the curtain walls surmounted by a watch path.

Inside the walled town, the collegiate Saint-Aubin church watches over narrow streets of fine town houses with ornate dormer windows, portals and turrets. On the 4th of April 1381 the second Treaty of Guérande was signed in the chapel of Notre-Dame-la-Blanche, consecrating Duke Jean IV of Montfort.

Saint-Aubin collegiate church

Romanesque and Gothic, the Saint-Aubin collegiate church combines majesty and light. The south façade attracts ones attention by the elegant lines of the gables and its Flamboyant porch. Inside, the statues, recumbent statues, stained glass windows and capitals are a rich and diversified mix of styles and ages.

BATZ-SUR-MER

Between the ocean and the salt marshes, hemmed in on its narrow peninsula, Batz-sur-Mer, for a long time, has lived on the salt exploited on the four hundred hectares of salt pans by the paludiers (salt workers) and sold by the sauniers (salt merchants).

The town has two sanctuaries: the Flamboyant Gothic Saint-Guénolé church whose sixty-metre-high spire dominates the region, and the Notre-Dame-du Mûrier chapel, in ruins since 1820. A gracious statue by Jean Fréour marks the entrance to the Salt marshes museum.

THE SALT MARSHES

The Pouliguen etier (sea water canal) brings sea water to the salt marshes, a fascinating puzzle of basins (oeillets) punctuated by white mole-hill-like piles of salt (mûlons). The water follows its surprising course allowing it, little by little, to evaporate and the salt to crystallise. At the end of the day, the salt worker (paludier) gathers the salt with his enormous flat rake, the las. During local pardons and festivals salt workers wear the traditional dress of baggy breeches, colourful waistcoat and large felt hat.

Plan of a salt pan

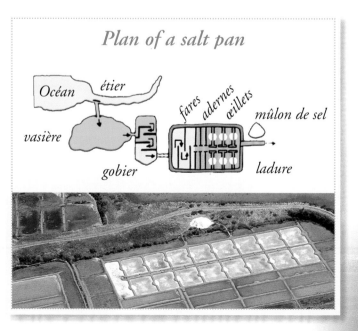

Océan · étier · fares · adernes · œillets · mûlon de sel · vasière · gobier · ladure

LE CROISIC

It is without doubt one of Brittany's most beautiful ports, with its succession of docks, the "chambres", opening onto the Grand Traict, the sea water channel leading to the salt marshes. Lined with 17th century town houses with wrought iron balconies and dormer windows, dominated by the classic belfry of Notre-Dame-de-Pitié (rebuilt during the reign of Louis XIV to rivalise with the one in Batz), the quays still echo with the glorious seafaring past of Le Croisic. They talk of salt exportation, of cod, sardine, herring and whaling.

Facing the port, the swirling winged ballet of seagulls.

More recently, during the last century, they remember the first canning factories, the first tourists (ever since the Restoration!), the port and its Bigouden seamen and their wives, the lacemakers. Facing the sea, the rocks along the "wild coast", sometimes with strange unexpected shapes, are constantly pounded by the waves.

Along the quays of Le Croisic, houses of former ship owners remind us of the prosperous fishing and trading past of the town.

The Croisic Océarium

With its star fish like architecture, the Le Croisic Océarium offers a fascinating plunge into the rich and diversified fauna of the Atlantic. Its tunnel-aquarium gives the visitor the impression of being amongst the sharks, rays and all the other species present. A tropical room has a collection of fish from warmer waters, whilst outside lives a playful colony of penguins.

The "grande côte" of Le Croisic.

The Bear Rock.

LA BAULE

From 1879 onwards, amongst shady dunes, along the immense eight kilometre beach, served by the railway, a new holiday resort began to develop.

From the original modest village of Escoublac, La Baule became an internationally known resort. Financiers and urban planners laid out avenues and the coastal boulevard, built palaces, constructed villages amongst the trees. Everything is opulent, chic and in good taste.

La Baule beach.

The casino, the Thalago sea water therapy institute and the Royal Hotel.

Summer firework display.

Since then La Baule has become more democratic and modern apartment buildings have colonised the sea front, but the older residential quarters still have that deliciously antiquated atmosphere of late 19th century seaside resort architecture.

L'étier (sea water canal leading to the salt marshes).

Early morning horse-riding along La Baule beach.

LE POULIGUEN

To the west of La Baule's main beach, Le Pouliguen is everything but a recently created resort. At the entrance of the channel leading to the salt marshes, it was an important fishing port as far back as the Middle Ages. If traditional fishermen's houses still exist in the main centre, the canal, now a marina, is lined with modern buildings.

PORNICHET

It was the initiative of a ship owner from Nantes and Parisian publishers, including Camille Flammarion, that led to the resort's development from 1860 onwards. Hotels and villas were built among the dunes and pine woods along the eastern side of Pouliguen Bay. Pornichet's pride and glory is that its development began about twenty years before La Baule. Its marina is curiously situated in open water, as if ready to slip its moorings and set sail.

Les Océanes, the town centre's dolphin, the marina and the coast towards Saint-Marguerite.

LA BRIÈRE

ere is a world apart, secret, soaked in water, criss-crossed by canals, inhabited by wild birds. In the central part, the seven thousand hectares of the Grand Brière, jointly owned by the twenty one communes around it, forms a Regional Nature Park since 1970. It is important to protect France's second largest marshland area (the Camargue is the largest), and also, if possible, allow it to live and develop normally. In the past, turf cutting, reeds, animal rearing, hunting and fishing provided a livelihood for local families. Today, it would be regrettable if tourism only maintained a seasonal activity. Therefore, the Park authorities help and encourage the local population with advice on tourism, renovation of the local habitat etc, and try to find new outlets and markets for traditional activities.

A peaceful trip in a flat-bottomed boat along a canal flanked by reeds.

In the heart of the marshlands, the island of Fédrun has carefully restored thatched cottages around the central gagnerie, the area reserved for cereal crops. One of these cottages, open to the public, is an attractive popular arts museum. All around, a canal, the *curée*, gave everyone a place to moor his boat.

The carefully restored village of Kerhinet houses a small museum of Brière traditional arts. From the port of Bréca one can take a boat trip around this spongy, bewitching world which has remained apart from the bustle of modern life. A world to discover at the slow rhythm of flat-bottomed boats among the reeds and rushes.

In the past, flat-bottomed boats were used for both eel fishing and transporting peat and reeds.

Eel fishing

Peat cutting in the Brière led to the creation of hollows invaded by water, locally called "piardes". These are excellent "pimpeneaux" (local name for eels) fishing grounds. Boats leave from the ports of Bréca, La Chaussée Neuve, Fédrun and Rozé to fish eel, using a short rake, the "foëne", whose teeth are used to trap the eels.

For the gourmet, fresh water crayfish.

SAINT-NAZAIRE

On the Loire estuary, Saint-Nazaire, audaciously rebuilt after the last war, is a town that lives by and for the sea. The small 19th century town of six hundred inhabitants has become France's fourth most important port! Its Atlantic Shipyards impress as much by their gigantic installations as by the elegant thoroughbred beauty of the ships built there, especially the modern cruise liners. The museum retraces the epic period of the Transat, when the town was one of Europe's bridgeheads to the New World. Discover life abroad the submarine L'Espadon, built in 1959 and the first to sail through the Antarctic ice caps. When the port's lights sparkle in the night, Saint-Nazaire's roadstead becomes a mirror of haloed poetry. The 3356 metres long Saint-Nazaire Bridge offers a splendid view over the Loire estuary and its two contrasting sides, industrial to the north, holiday resorts (Saint-Brévin-les-Pins) to the south. The bridge's central span is over sixty metres above the water.

The port of Saint-Nazaire illuminated. Light artist: Yann Kersalé.

The submarine base

This gigantic bunker, 301 metres long, 18 metres high, was built between January 1941 and December 1942, using 480,000 cubic metres or reinforced concrete. Two fleets of U. Boote (Wegener and Hundius) used it as a maintenance and torpedo rearming base in between Atlantic patrols. It wasn't until the 10th of May 1945 that the German General Junck accepted the surrender of the Saint-Nazaire Pocket. A vast new project called "l'Escale Atlantique" has been launched to rehabilitate this enormous area.

The Atlantic Shipyards

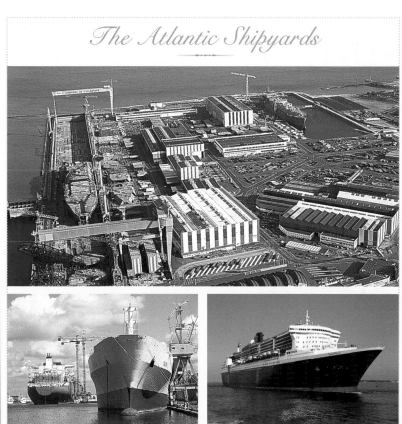

SAINT-MARC-SUR-MER

For all cinema fans, the beach at Saint-Marc-sur-Mer will forever remain as the setting for the *Vacances de M. Hulots*. In 1951, Jacques Tati chose the Hôtel de la Plage of this quiet resort as the setting for his famous film. It is easy to see why the film-maker was attracted to the family atmosphere of its beach of fine sand flanked by yellow-coloured cliffs.

NANTES

The nave and choir of Nantes's Saint-Pierre cathedral.

Whatever the degree of Breton conscientiousness claimed by its inhabitants, Nantes will remain forever as the capital of the Duchy of Brittany at its apogee and its final lament. Inside its medieval walls, which used to stand in the waters of the Loire, François II and later his daughter Anne built the impressive grand logis in a the sparkling Renaissance style still influenced by the Flamboyant Gothic. Rebuilt in the 15th century on the site of a former Romanesque sanctuary (a crypt still remains), the Saint-Pierre cathedral has been painstakingly restored after the fire in 1972. Inside, the elegant verticality of the pillars is flooded with light. The absolute masterpiece of Breton statue art, the tomb of Duke François II and his wife Marguerite de Foix, is the work of Michel Colombe. What grace and power in the recumbent figures of white marble and the four corner statues incarnating the four Cardinal Virtues!

The former course of the River Erdre separates the medieval quarters of the town from the 18th and 19th century parts. The place Royale, the square and quarter of Graslin, the Crucy theatre are all illustrations of the apotheosis of Classical urban planning a few years prior to the French Revolution. The three levels of the Pommeraye Passage decorated with dream-like statues is the most magical example of a covered passage that 19th century France has to offer. It is easy to understand why it was praised by and inspired many an artist, from the film director Jacques Demy, the writer Pieyre de Mandiargues, to the comic strip illustrator Tardi.

The tomb of François II.

140

Nantes's Saint-Pierre cathedral.

By the river and along its former course, unfortunately filled in between the two wars, on Feydeu island and along the Fosse quays, imposing town houses of former ship owners, crowned with pediments and adorned with carved figures, take us back to another more talked about episode of Nantes's past: the era when great fortunes were made through the slave trade. The metropolis of the Pays de Loire, still nostalgic of its ducal past, knows that its futures lies in a harmonious synthesis of its double identity, between Leaguer and Breton.

CHÂTEAUBRIANT

At the limit of the Ille-et-Vilaine and Anjou, the Mée pays has escaped the modern touristic flow. This is regrettable for Châteaubriant, its capital, whose Renaissance castle seems to be transplanted from the banks of the Loire into the quiet Breton countryside. Its Italian style gallery with arcades and schist columns, its dormer windows surmounted by pediments and candelabra, its balconied staircase, all at Châteaubriant takes us back to an art of living that wanted to change from the somber medieval heritage outside.

Its designer, Jean de Laval, Governor of Brittany, was married to Françoise de Foix, cousin of Anne of Brittany… and mistress of François I for eight years. Laval didn't hold it against her and in 1532 began to build this delightful residence, a hymn to his refound love.

Châteaubriant Castle, owned by the Loire-Atlantique Conseil Général (County Council), is a listed historical monument.

The ramparts and the grand logis of Nantes Castle.

The Ar-Men lighthouse, keeping watch at the end of the earth.